The Top Ten Myths of American Health Care
A Citizen's Guide

By Sally C. Pipes

with a foreword by Steve Forbes

PRi

PACIFIC
RESEARCH
INSTITUTE

To my husband Charles Kesler and Maggie who never seem to tire
of my endless ruminations on health care

The Top Ten Myths of American Health Care: A Citizen's Guide
By Sally C. Pipes

ISBN-13: 978-1-934276-12-9
October 2008 | $19.95

Library of Congress Catalog-in-Publication Data

Pacific Research Institute
One Embarcadero Center, Suite 350
San Francisco, CA 94111
Tel: 415-989-0833/ 800-276-7600
Fax: 415-989-2411
Email: info@pacificresearch.org
www.pacificresearch.org

10 9 8 7 6 5 4 3

Additional print copies of this book may be purchased by
contacting us at the address above, or download the PDF
version at www.pacificresearch.org.

Nothing contained in this report is to be construed as necessarily
reflecting the views of the Pacific Research Institute or as an attempt
to thwart or aid the passage of any legislation.

Contents

Foreword

This is the right book at the right time. As I write this, the presidential campaign is in full swing—and health care reform is one of the most contentious issues. The American electorate is about to choose leaders who will make critical policy decisions regarding an area that will soon absorb a full 20 percent of our country's economy.

The path this country takes in the next year will have an incalculable impact, not just on the future of health care in America, but on the fundamental relationship between government and free enterprise in our society.

With this book, Sally Pipes gives us an invaluable tool for navigating the health care debate. But she doesn't simply debunk ten popular myths. She puts lasting insights down on the table for whenever citizens and policymakers must deal with the seductive, but dangerous, argument that only government is able to provide essential economic goods and services to its people.

This important little book goes beyond the issue of raising taxes to pay for what politicians so often imply is free. It takes a hard look at how governments actually spend the money they take from the productive economy. What value do the recipients of government largesse get for each federal dollar and what are the real costs to society?

Recognizing that no delivery system is perfect or even totally fair, Sally Pipes strips away the soaring rhetoric used by today's politicians. She looks closely at the real record of government, not just in American health care, but, around the world. She shows us how massive government intervention has actually performed and the many policy quagmires it has created.

But this is also a "fix-it" book. It uncovers the real problems with the U.S. health care system—and then offers practical ways to solve those problems. *The Top Ten Myths of American Health Care* opens the door to commonsense alternatives that every American should understand.

For anyone interested in getting to the core of America's health-care troubles, this is the perfect book. And for health care policy makers, it should be required reading. Sally Pipes presents options that are are simpler, more flexible, and more responsive to people's needs and desires than the politically-driven panacea of government spending.

If you instinctively question the need for government control over yet another aspect of our lives, but feel the health care "crisis" is too complicated to fathom, then read on.

Steve Forbes
New York, New York

Acknowledgements

I would like to thank the following individuals for their contributions to this book: Sam Ryan and Lloyd Billingsley for their fine editing and Linda Bridges for her copyediting skills; Denise Tsui, PRI's talented graphic designer; Diana Ernst who helped me with the extensive research required for this book; Rowena Itchon, PRI's vice president of marketing for her tireless work on constantly improving the project; and Keybridge Communications for their help in promotion. I also thank those scholars and health care experts who have encouraged and contributed to PRI's work in this area.

I am especially grateful to my friend Steve Forbes for writing the foreword to this book.

Very special thanks also go the contributors to the Pacific Research Institute, who made my work on this project possible. I am tremendously appreciative of your intellectual, as well as financial support.

Any errors or omissions are my sole responsibility.

Sally C. Pipes

Introduction: Two Competing Visions for Health Care in America

Few issues in American politics capture more attention—and passion—than health care. Opinions vary widely about what's wrong with our current system. And there's even less consensus on how to fix it. But one thing we can all agree upon is that our health care system is in desperate need of reform. We all want affordable, accessible, high-quality health care.

Why is there such interest in fixing American health care? Because most of us realize that, sooner or later, the quality of our medical system will wield enormous impact on our own lives, or the lives of those we love.

Moreover, the growing cost of our system is placing a heavy financial burden on all of us. In 2007, insurance premiums rose at more than double the rate of inflation.[1] And health care spending, it is estimated, will consume as much as 20 percent of the U.S. economy by 2016—up from 16 percent in 2007.[2]

As these costs increase, our wallets get lighter. Wages stagnate as employer-provided health insurance gobbles up our paychecks. Most Americans realize—even if only instinctively—that today's health care system is simply not sustainable on its current cost trajectory.

So, on the simplest level, the question of how to reform the U.S. health care system boils down to this: How do we control costs without sacrificing quality? And how can we reach coverage that is universal, or at least nearly universal?

There are many answers to that question. But the vast majority of solutions proposed by today's politicians fall into one of two ideological camps:

The first camp maintains that only the government can cure our health care woes. Because the problem itself is massive and complex, we need an equally massive and complex solution. With sufficient taxpayer funding, the government has the size, infrastructure, and power to deliver that solution on a national scale. Uncle Sam has the wisdom and wherewithal to hold prices in check, while simultaneously ensuring that all Americans have access to high-quality health care.

The second camp believes that government is actually part of the problem. Too much regulation has caused our health care system to become sluggish, overpriced, and unresponsive to consumer demands. Rather than expand the government's role, we should reduce it—and instead foster free-market competition by empowering consumers. Why not let the same economic forces that have improved quality and lowered costs in almost every other industry—from cars to computers—flourish in health care?

As a nation, we're clearly split between these two camps. However, a growing percentage of Americans seem to lean toward the belief that the solution lies in more government. After all, more than half of all health care provided in this country already is paid for by the government through Medicare, Medicaid, the State Children's Health Insurance Program, and health insurance programs for veterans, Native Americans, and other specific populations. Over time, polls have shown that Americans favor greater government involvement in health care—or even an outright federal guarantee of health insurance for all.[3] It sure seems as if few Americans make the connection between government-provided health care and the Department of Motor Vehicles or the way government handled the devastation from Hurricane Katrina.

The debate is far from over. Polls also show that most Americans are personally satisfied with their own health coverage.[4] And most of us would prefer private insurance to a government-provided plan.

But now it seems that advocates of government-run health care have the upper hand. Perhaps it's because they're promising something that has always been a winner in political debates—a free lunch. Or more specifically, in this case, high-quality health care paid for by somebody else.

Like all utopian promises, the idea of free health care for all sounds wonderful. But what would this vision look like in reality? Is it true that our medical care can be saved by a massive intervention of government in the American economy?

The thesis of this book is that a government-run health care system would be an enormous mistake for America. It's an empty promise built upon a foundation of myths.

My goal in writing this book is to debunk those myths. Each chapter focuses on one of the 10 most popular myths in the health care debate. These are arguments made by politicians, policymakers, commentators, and journalists—myths that have been repeated so often that millions think they're true. I will give you—in plain English—arguments against massive government medical monopolies.

I will also outline some ways to achieve real health care reform— solutions that will cost less and be more effective in fixing the problems that plague our medical system, while also ensuring that American health care remains the best in the world.

Myth One: Government Health Care Is More Efficient

In August 2008, the prestigious British medical journal *Lancet Oncology*[1] published the results of an extraordinary study. The study found that America is much better at treating cancer than Europe or Canada.

As it turns out, Americans have a better survival rate for 13 of the 16 most common cancers. Among men, an American has nearly a 20-percent better chance of living for five years after being diagnosed with cancer than his European counterpart. American women stand a 7.2-percent better chance of living for five years after a cancer diagnosis than their European counterparts.

Perhaps that's one reason why tens of thousands of foreigners come to the United States every year for medical treatment. They're usually seeking advanced and sophisticated procedures that are simply unavailable—or rationed—in their home countries.

Surprised? That's because every time you pick up a newspaper or turn on the nightly news, someone is calling for the government to fix our health care system by creating a national, government-run program similar to the systems of Britain, Canada, or France. Many prominent pundits and lawmakers believe that only the government is big enough and powerful enough to fix our health care problems and provide affordable, accessible, quality care for all Americans.

Alas, these advocates of "universal care" have fallen victim to one of the most pervasive myths in America today—that government-run health care is effective and efficient. Nothing could be further from the truth.

Is Health Care a Right?

When serious illness strikes, or when life and death issues are at stake, it's understandable that people could be persuaded that health care is a "right." But in the same way that food, shelter, and clothing are not rights, neither is health care.

We do not have a God-given or government-secured right to any of these things, as critical as they are to our survival.

Some of the best minds today, from economists to physicians to politicians, believe that the United States, a free, just, and compassionate society—not to mention the richest nation in the world—should take on the responsibility of providing health care for everyone. Just think if we the public should accept this offer.

☞ Would you want to eat government-made food?

☞ Would you want to live in public housing?

☞ How about government-issued clothes?

☞ Are you game for a government-made car?

If you're like most Americans, your answer is "No, thank you."

Does the IRS make paying your taxes simpler?

Critics of America's health care system often cite the "cost of the middleman" when making their case.

This simplistic line of reasoning goes as follows: The more middlemen that stand between the producer of a service and the ultimate consumer, the more expensive that service will be, because each intermediary adds his own profit to the chain. Accordingly, it would be more rational—and cheaper—to have

A right to health care and other basic needs such as food, clothing, and shelter do not appear in any of America's founding documents such as the Declaration of Independence, the Constitution, or the Bill of Rights. Moreover, our rights, properly understood, are *not* granted by these founding documents. Rather, these documents were intended to limit the power of government and to *safeguard* our rights and freedoms.

When government gets involved in health care—in legislating who gets it, how it's used, and who's going to pay for it—government is actually limiting our rights and diminishing our freedom to access the health care we want. Moreover, as Robert Samuelson writes, "The trouble with casting medical-care as a "right" is that this ignores how open-ended the "right" should be and how fulfilling it might compromise other "rights" and needs. What makes people healthy or unhealthy are personal habits, good or bad (diet, exercise, alcohol, drug use); genetic makeup, lucky or unlucky, and age. Health care, no matter how lavishly provided, can only partially compensate for these individual differences."[2]

a single producer move services directly to consumers, eliminating the middleman.

Who would be that producer? The government of course. Advocates of nationalized health care contend that the government could simplify the production of health care goods and services, provide more efficient coverage, and lower costs.

It's easy to see how such an argument could take hold. It *seems* right. It *seems* logical. But is it true?

Think about it. Does the IRS make paying your taxes simpler? Do government-run schools provide the best K–12 education? In fact, do *current* state and federal regulations make our health care better and more efficient?

The answer, obviously, is "no." Almost without exception, *wherever* government intervenes to solve a major social problem—despite good intentions—the affected process becomes enormously more complicated and much more expensive for society as a whole. And, health care and K–12 education are the two sectors in America that have more government involvement than any other and they both suffer from serious quality problems.

The thicket of government "middlemen"

There is ample evidence that *government itself* is the middleman.

Over the last few decades, state and federal lawmakers have instituted a confusing patchwork of restrictions and regulations in an attempt to drive down costs. However, these moves actually have increased health care costs and made it impossible for private enterprise to work effectively. Empowerment—putting doctors and patients in charge of their health care—would be far more efficient.

Consider insurance. Today, insurers who want to make health care policies available to the public have to be registered and reviewed by 50 different state insurance administrations. Consumers are barred from purchasing policies across state lines, making it impossible for individuals and families to get the type of insurance plan that best meets their needs in terms of coverage and cost.

And most states force residents to buy one-size-fits-all insurance packages that include all sorts of services that only a small slice of the population needs. The average state imposes 38 mandates on an individual health insurance policy. In 2007, there were 1,901 different mandates nationwide. These extraneous mandates increase the price of basic insurance by as much as 50 percent.[3]

Insurers also have to deal with overlapping federal regulations. Indeed, insurance companies are so hobbled by government regulations that they have to hire legions of lawyers just to keep up.

Real costs pushed onto the private sector

Critics of the U.S. system often argue that Medicare and other government programs have lower administrative costs than private health insurance. According to the most recent Medicare Trustees Report, administrative costs for Medicare are only 1.5 percent of total expenditures.[4] For private health care, that number is said to be as high as 25 percent.

Walk into any hospital or doctor's office and you will see why these estimates are misleading and inaccurate. According to a recent study by the Council for Affordable Health Insurance, the administrative costs of Medicare actually total around 5.2 percent. Meanwhile, the administrative costs of private-sector health care total about 8.9 percent. A similar study by PricewaterhouseCoopers found that only 6 percent of private health care premiums go to administrative costs and a full 86 percent of premiums go to providing actual medical care.[5] The reason that official estimates were so far off was that they didn't account for Medicare's hidden costs.[6]

For instance, the Medicare Trustees report doesn't include things like the salaries of managers and administrators or the marketing costs associated with advertising new policies like the Medicare Part D drug benefit. Private health care providers, on the other hand, include all of these expenses in their estimates of administrative costs.

On top of that, Medicare passes off a great deal of its costs to private payers. A recent study showed that, in Washington State alone, $738 million in charges were shifted to private payers to make up for underpayments by Medicare and Medicaid in 2004. That same year in California, private payers and hospitals paid an extra $45 billion to compensate for unpaid Medicare costs.[7]

Indeed, even though proponents of government health care insist that the uninsured represent a "hidden tax"—that is, those with health insurance pay a hidden tax to subsidize the care of those without health insurance—the reality is that the "uninsured" add only about 1 percent in hidden costs to the price of the insured's insurance plan. A far greater hidden tax is caused by government Medicare and Medicaid programs' low reimbursement rates which add as much as 10 percent in hidden costs, or subsidies, to those paying for private health insurance.[8]

Do single payers equal lower prices?

Advocates of socialized medicine often claim that when the government—as single payer to all providers—runs the till, it can negotiate lower prices up and down the line. If economic history has taught us anything, however, it's that government price controls have been an unmitigated disaster every time they have been applied beginning with Emperor Diocletian's edict in Rome in 301.[9]

During World War II, federal lawmakers instituted price controls on a wide range of goods and services. But the government needed an enormous amount of muscle to enforce the new rules, so it created an independent Office of Price Administration—and granted the agency the authority to place price ceilings on everything except agricultural commodities and to ration anything that was scarce. At its height, the agency had nearly 65,000 employees on its payroll, and another 100,000 volunteer "price watchers" across the country. By war's end, it had filed nearly 260,000 lawsuits to enforce the price ceilings.

Nonetheless, a lucrative black market emerged for everything from cars to underwear. Businesses that didn't go underground cut costs by lowering the quality of their products. A 1943 study from *Consumer Reports*, for instance, tested 20 candy bars and found that 19 had shrunk in size from four years earlier.

Put simply, those price controls resulted in a number of unintended consequences. And they were just *temporary*. In the Soviet Union, where state control of the economy was a permanent fixture, consumers were forced to stand in long lines for the barest necessities.

Price controls are, however, quite effective in limiting innovation. For health care, this would be disastrous.

Just take pharmaceuticals. Behind each pill's price tag is time and money that went toward research and development. R&D is a huge investment—on average, it now takes about $1.3 billion to bring a single drug to the market.[10]

The market price for drugs reflects these risky investments and provides an incentive for researchers to keep coming up with new cures. Government-mandated prices do not. Quite literally, the difference is a matter of life and death.

Researchers at the University of Connecticut Center for Health-care and Insurance Studies recently found that government interference in drug pricing has caused $188 billion in lost R&D spending since 1960. That money would have gone to develop new, perhaps life-saving, medicines. These "lost" medicines could have saved 140 million life years.

Government health care—it's already here

In 1965, two massive government health care programs were launched—Medicare and its late entrant, Medicaid. This federal intrusion into the health care system has distorted the entire market ever since and yet politicians keep calling for expanding these "excellent" programs to cover all Americans, "Medicare for all" as Senator Ted Kennedy (D-MA) likes to call it.

Medicare, the primary insurance program for Americans over the age of 65, is funded entirely by the federal government, i.e. taxpayers. In fiscal year 2007, Medicare spent $427 billion accounting for 16 percent of the federal budget. This year, Medicare will spend more than it collects from payroll taxes and by 2017, it will spend $884 billion. It will take a payroll tax of 6.4 percent just to keep the program afloat.[11]

Wasting away

We've already seen how Medicare passes much of its costs off to private payers. But it also wastes an enormous amount of money. Studies show that Medicare officials waste as much as $1 out of every $3 the program spends.[12] That's hardly a system worth expanding.

Medicaid, the insurance program for poor Americans, is administered at the state level and receives about 50 to 70 percent of its funding from the federal government. It, too, is a model of inefficiency. And there's an enormous amount of fraud. The total federal state cost of Medicaid in 2007 was $338 billion and is projected to be $717 billion in 2017.[13]

In New York State alone, a retired chief fraud investigator estimates that as much as 40 percent of the state's Medicaid claims are fraudulent. This costs the state about $18 billion a year.[14] Examples of fraud abound. In 2003, for example, Dr. Dolly Rosen billed Medicaid for 991 procedures *each day*, costing taxpayers more than $1 million.[15]

Both Medicare and Medicaid also impose price controls by setting low reimbursement rates to doctors and hospitals. This has caused an enormous amount of hardship, as an increasing number of doctors are refusing to see patients if the government is footing the bill. Nearly one in three seniors in search of a new doctor is struggling to do so, according to the Medicare Payment Advisory Commission.[16] "When I moved down here, I thought the only difficulty would be in finding good ones," reported a newly enrolled Medicare patient about finding a doctor in Raleigh, N.C. "but it turned out that I would call a place and say, 'I have Med--' and they wouldn't even let me finish."[17]

The government may efficiently control the costs at which doctors are reimbursed. This does not, however, account for the pain and suffering people endure waiting for care or the value of their time spent searching for a doctor. The government sets the fees paid to doctors according to a schedule of codes for 8,000 procedures. The cost is $60 billion.[18]

According to a recent report from the Center for the Study of Health System Change, just about half of all doctors said they had stopped seeing or limited the number of new Medicaid patients.[19]

Expansion continues

Despite these realities, the expansion of government health care continues.

In 1997, the State Children's Health Insurance Program (SCHIP) was established with the noble goal of providing health insurance to low-income children in households with low incomes that nonetheless exceed Medicaid eligibility. Today, SCHIP covers about six million children.[20]

The program's funding formula, however, gave states an incentive to add middle-income children and even adults to their SCHIP rolls. So in many places, the program spiraled out of control. In 14 states, adults are enrolled in SCHIP; nationwide, about 600,000 adults are covered by the program. In six states, more SCHIP money is spent on adults than on kids. Meanwhile, the program has still failed to enroll almost two million children who qualify.

Instead of focusing on getting these kids to enroll, lawmakers attempted to expand the program in 2007—seeking to offer

---

Hassles Force a Retreat from Military Families

"After four years of providing care to military personnel, their families, and retirees, I've had it." The hassles of working with the Tricare program that covers health care for these people got the better of me. I've taken care of about 80 Tricare patients. But I won't be seeing them anymore....Early on I began to understand what a tough job treating Tricare patients was going to be. One woman needed a colorectal surgeon ....The specialized surgeons in our region weren't in the network, and the closest Tricare doctors who could help her were in Indiana. She traveled out of state to get her problem fixed. When she had complications following her operation, I ended up managing her surgical skin infection because the surgeon was three hours away. Everything about her case required special arrangements—emails to Tricare, faxes to Tricare, and my nurse holding on the phone to Tricare....I felt isolated and ineffective navigating the roadblocks in the Tricare system just to get basic care ...for my patients. It seemed too often that I was doctoring with one hand tied behind my back."

—Benjamin Brewer, MD, *The Wall Street Journal* online.[21]

SCHIP to families earning up to 300 percent of the federal poverty level. President George W. Bush vetoed the measure.

The Department of Veterans Affairs (VA) also runs a government health care program. Like Medicare, Medicaid, and SCHIP, it too is sometimes trotted out as evidence that government-run health care can actually work.

But thus far, the VA has proved inadequate for the many wounded veterans who have returned home from Iraq and Afghanistan. Better suited to the needs of much older veterans from World War II, Korea, and Vietnam, the VA is simply unable to react with the speed and efficacy needed to deal with the injuries of modern warfare.

A claim now takes between 127 and 177 days to process—well above the private industry average, which is 89.5. An appeal takes a staggering 657 days. In House testimony last year, the Government Accountability Office (GAO) reported that the VA is near the breaking point.

The 60-ton nail

Back in the days of total state economic planning in the communist countries of Eastern Europe, there was a widely circulated anecdote. The government wanted to produce more nails and set a *nail quota* for each factory. One factory was ordered to produce 60 tons of nails. At the end of the year, the factory made its quota. It rolled out *one* 60-ton nail!

Silly, of course. But the joke circulated because it captured so well the essence of how top-down planning is routinely manipulated and distorted to the point of economic insanity. The reality behind stories like this one is the reason the communist system collapsed. Too few real nails ever made it to consumers.

Myth Two: We're Spending Too Much on Health Care.

It's easy to think that health care spending is out of control.

In 1950, the average American spent about $500 a year on health care in 2006 inflation-adjusted dollars.[1] Back then, health care costs accounted for a mere 5 percent of GDP.[2]

By 2006, those same costs had risen to $7,026 per person, and accounted for 16 percent of GDP.[3]

Even over the span of a half century, that's a pretty eye-popping increase. So it's not hard to understand why Americans have gone from merely griping about doctors' bills to raising their voices in an increasingly loud chorus of complaints.

America's leaders have come under enormous pressure to devise a political solution to rein in rising health care costs. And many politicians are now talking about dramatic overhauls to our current system. Some are even calling for a government takeover of health care—essentially expanding programs like Medicare and Medicaid to the entire U.S. population.

But before we hop on the "universal care" bandwagon, a reality check is in order.

The simple fact is that we are *not* paying too much for health care in this country.

Paying with your life

In the health care debate today, rapidly rising costs are a common refrain. Yet, you'll almost never hear anyone talk about the dramatic increase in *value* that Americans have derived from their health care over the last 50 years.

As any economist could tell you, there's a big difference between *cost* and *value*. And, in fact, it can be the difference between life and death.

A friend of mine is a young man named Chad Wilkinson. In 1998, at the age of 25, Chad was diagnosed with non-Hodgkin's lymphoma (NHL). The doctors told him that, statistically, he had a 35 percent chance of surviving. Today, Chad is in excellent health. He owes his life to the miracles of modern medicine.

"When people say that health care in the United States has too high a cost, I just assume they've never been in a fight to the death with cancer," says Chad. "My chemo bills were through the roof, but that treatment was worth every nickel. If some bean-counting bureaucrat were calling the shots, my health care would have been free, but the quality would have been inferior—and I'd probably be dead."

What Chad understands instinctively is that words like "cost" and "value" can't simply be measured in dollars. As he says, "The cost isn't low if you end up paying with your life."[4]

Moreover, when we talk about re-tooling our health care, we should be careful to also recognize what is good about the current system. Most everyone has a friend or relative who is alive today because of an advance—probably a very expensive advance—in medical technology or drugs.

Don't forget the life-saving benefits

Jonas Salk's life-saving polio vaccine is more than 50 years old. Up until that time you didn't need to spend much on medicine to prevent polio. There simply weren't any effective therapies available.

Since that time, however—in the last half a century or so—we've seen advances in medicine occurring so fast that only specialized, full-time medical professionals can keep up.

Unfortunately, the life-saving benefits of these advances are often forgotten when it comes time to pay for them.

People may not want to recognize that such advances are not free.

Perhaps no one has explained this more clearly than Dr. David Gratzer, a practicing Canadian physician and senior fellow at the Manhattan Institute. In his excellent book, *The Cure: How Capitalism Can Save American Health Care*, Dr. Gratzer uses the example of cardiac care. The clot-busting drug tPA costs thousands of dollars per use; bypass surgery costs tens of thousands of dollars; and a pacemaker roughly $20,000 to $25,000.

It costs money to keep people alive. But it's money well spent.

"Let's put this figure in perspective," Dr. Gratzer notes. "The little box in the chest of [Vice President Dick Cheney] costs more than fifty times what the average American spent on health care (adjusted for inflation) for an entire year in 1950."[5]

Medical Specialties Hit by a Growing Pay Gap

"As a neuro-ophthalmologist, Larry Frohman diagnoses unusual visual problems and many complex nervous disorders that often baffle other doctors. He's also part of an endangered species. Over the next decade, roughly 140 of the country's remaining 400 neuro-ophthalmologists— trained to detect and treat visual problems connected to the brain—will have reached retirement age according to an analysis of the North American Neuro-Ophthalmology Society's membership roster. Yet only 20 medical residents have opted to enter the field in the past four years, according to the society….Many in health-policy circles have focused on how the current health-care payment system is helping create shortages among primary-care doctors, internists, and others on the front lines of medicine. But often lost is how the system is endangering some of the country's most highly trained specialists as well."

—Vanessa Fuhrmans, *Wall Street Journal*.[6]

We spend more because it's worth it

Of course, none of these life-saving advances in cardiac care was available half-a-century ago. People didn't spend money on health care largely because there was little to spend it on. We pay more for health care today because the treatments are there and they work.

American life expectancy increased by about 30 years over the course of the twentieth century. If you were a male born in 1900, there was an 18-percent chance you'd be dead by your first birthday. As of 2005, the cumulative mortality rate doesn't reach 18 percent until age 62.[7]

Meanwhile, from 1950 to 2000, the death rate from heart disease—America's number one killer—was reduced by 59 percent, from 307 to 126 deaths per 100,000.[8] In a single decade, from 1993 to 2003, heart disease deaths dropped 22 percent.[9]

So while it's true that we're paying 14 times as many dollars for health care as we did in 1950, we're getting an amazing return on our investment. Since 1950, the average U.S. life expectancy has increased by almost nine years.

Measuring lives

How much would you pay for an extra nine years of life? Can you put a price tag on such a thing? Some economists have tried. They've come up with some fancy equations that at least take a stab at putting price tags on imponderables like "life" and "health."

In a remarkable study, University of Chicago economists Kevin M. Murphy and Robert Topel developed "an economic framework for valuing improvements to health and life expectancy, based on individuals' willingness to pay."[10]

What they discovered was something that my friend Chad Wilkinson knew instinctively. There is enormous and unrecognized value in medicine that goes way beyond the dollars we pay to our doctors and hospitals.

In fact, Murphy and Topel concluded that longevity gains as a result of medical innovations are currently worth $2.8 trillion annually. That's larger than the GDP of the United Kingdom.[11]

"The historical gains from increased longevity have been enormous. Over the twentieth century, cumulative gains in life expectancy were worth over $1.2 million *per person* for both men and women."[12]

Further, even marginal gains resulting from medical innovations are astonishingly high. A 1-percent reduction in cancer mortality would bring a life value of $500 billion.

Of course, such numbers are certainly debatable. But as Murphy and Topel conclude "these estimates indicate that the social returns to investment in new medical knowledge are enormous."[13] That is, perhaps, an understatement.

Free magic pills?

If you were on death's doorstep and I offered you a $20,000 pill that would give you another 20 years of life, would you say it's too expensive?

Probably not.

If you break down the cost, it comes out to just $1,000 per extra year of life. Most Americans would call that a pretty good deal.

Unfortunately, most Americans aren't accustomed to thinking about medicine in that way. That's because we don't usually pay for our health care directly, instead buying subsidized insurance through our employers.

As a result, we tend to think that medicine isn't subject to the same laws of economics as other things we buy, like cars. We're perfectly happy to pay $20,000—or far more—for a new Honda.

But when it comes to paying for medicine—which is arguably of much greater value, particularly if you're really sick—we complain that it's too expensive.

A prescription medication, for example, might seem simple, but it can be just as complex as an automobile—from the research, to the testing, to the production. True, you can't buy a pill with power-steering and leather seats. But it can take just as much—if not more—money to develop.

Unfortunately, medical innovations don't just fall from heaven. They are the fruits of enormously expensive research and development efforts. Such efforts, in turn, depend on market forces that foster and reward innovation.

Today, the U.S. market for medical innovation is robust. Americans for the most part get cutting-edge care because we demand it and are willing to pay for it. Those miraculous advances may be costly, but as we've seen, they add life value and contribute to the buoyancy of the whole American economy—just as innovations in the automobile industry do. We get what we pay for.

We can afford it

Nonetheless, year-over-year increases in health care costs alarm us. We have a tendency to focus on such increases without putting them in perspective. The vast majority of Americans have no trouble paying for health care even though few politicians make that obvious point. In fact, we could even afford to pay much more for health care than we do now.

Health care spending today accounts for 16 percent of GDP. That figure includes the combined total of private insurance and government spending, a fact which obscures exactly how much Americans are paying *out of pocket* for health care.

The typical American family spends just 5.4 percent of its income on health care, as opposed to 40.8 percent on housing, 18.3 percent on transportation, and 18.2 percent on food.

In fact, the nearest comparable expense for families is the 4.5 percent of income spent on clothing.[14] And yet, we don't hear politicians calling for sweeping legislation to put price controls on textiles because every American has a right to designer fashions.

In short, the increases in overall health care costs—dramatic as they may seem—must be weighed relative to the huge increases in income and purchasing power Americans have enjoyed over the last half century. In a country where consumption spending finds so many and varied outlets, it's hard to see how spending on health care is somehow a unique problem.

More bang for the buck

In a 2007 paper for *The Quarterly Journal of Economics*, "The Value of Life and the Rise in Health Spending," economists Robert E. Hall and Charles I. Jones examine the factors affecting health spending.[15] Looking forward, they conclude that American spending on health care will approximately double over the next forty years so that the proportion of GDP devoted to health care will reach 33 percent by 2050.

But while spending twice as much on health care may seem daunting, the reality is not nearly so scary. According to Hall and Jones, "The account that emerges is that the marginal utility of non-health consumption diminishes faster than the marginal utility of health spending. As a result, the composition of total spending shifts toward health. The health share continues to grow as long as income grows."[16]

In everyday language, that means we're going to spend more on health than on other goods and services because we are getting, so to speak, more bang for the buck. As we earn more, we're likely to spend money on health care not because we "have to," but because we "want to."

Hall and Jones put it this way: "As we grow older and richer, which is more valuable: a third car, yet another television, more clothing—or an extra year of life?"[17] Thus, more spending on health care is the inevitable result of progress.

Keeping costs in perspective

In this country, medical care doesn't come cheap. But that doesn't mean it's too expensive—or that we're not getting our money's worth. The simple fact is, Americans are not spending too much for health care, just as we're not spending too much on clothes, food, and transportation.

This isn't to say that we don't need reform. There are many inefficiencies in our health care system that are driving costs up unnecessarily. And any number of sensible reforms could and should be enacted to keep health care prices down. These reforms are outlined in the final chapter of this book.

But as the health care reform debate rages, it's important to keep costs in perspective. Today, the average American has little trouble accessing a medical system that is saving lives and increasing our quality of life in ways unthinkable just a few years ago. It's important to keep that in mind when critics say we spend too much on it.

Myth Three: Forty-Six Million Americans Can't Get Health Care

 Forty-six million Americans—including nearly eight million children—lack health insurance with no signs of this trend slowing down. – Official Barack Obama website[1]

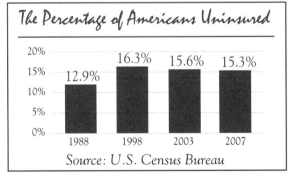

The Percentage of Americans Uninsured

Source: U.S. Census Bureau

Google the phrase "46 million uninsured," and you'll get about 25,000 hits.[2] It's one of the most widely-used statistics in the debate over health care reform.

Look up the term "uninsured" in Wikipedia, and the second sentence states: "In 2007, there were 45.7 million people in the U.S. (15.3 percent of the population) who were without health insurance for at least part of that year, according to the United States Census Bureau."[3]

This Census Bureau (CB) statistic is repeated *ad nauseum*—particularly by advocates of government monopoly heath care who claim that the main problem with America's health system is the massive uninsured population. After all, if a whopping 15 percent of the population is uninsured, then the current system must be failing.

And if private insurance companies can't get the job done, then surely only the government can. In other words, the federal government should step in and create a national health insurance plan to end this so-called crisis of the uninsured.

But is it really a crisis? Where does this Census Bureau statistic come from—and what exactly does it mean?

The answers may surprise you.

While it's not technically wrong to say that there are roughly 45.7 million uninsured, it's grossly misleading to use this number as an indication of a crisis.

More important, this statistic has led to the widespread belief that there are 45.7 million people in this country who can't afford health insurance—and don't have access to health care. In Canada, where there are just 33 million residents,[4] most people believe that the 45.7 million uninsured Americans have never had access to health insurance or health care.

Nothing could be further from the truth.

Understanding the Census Bureau's survey

Let's begin by examining how this statistic was generated. The Census Bureau relies entirely on a questionnaire known as the

Current Population Survey (CPS) for gathering information on health insurance. The survey is intended to garner information about, among many things, the income, age, race, living situation, and, of course, health insurance status of individuals living in the United States.

As with any survey of this size and scope, the accuracy of the data it produces has substantial margins of error. And this is especially true with the health insurance data collected via the CPS.

As the Census Bureau explains in its annual report *Income, Poverty, and Health Insurance Coverage in the United States* "health insurance coverage is likely to be underreported on the CPS."[5] The report goes on to say that "underreporting of health insurance coverage . . . appears to be a larger problem [in the CPS] than in other national surveys that ask about health insurance."

To its credit, the Census Bureau acknowledges that insurance coverage may be significantly higher than its data indicate.

What does the number mean?

Okay, so the data aren't necessarily exact. But let's assume for a moment that they're spot-on. What does it mean when the Census Bureau reports 45.7 million uninsured? Many people assume the Census Bureau is telling us that 45.7 million people are chronically uninsured for an entire year or more.

That's not the case at all. As the Census Bureau itself states, "the CPS estimate of the number of people without health insurance more closely approximates the number of people who are uninsured at a specific point in time during the year than the number of people uninsured for the entire year."[6]

In other words, many of the survey respondents who were counted as "uninsured" may have experienced only a temporary interruption in their insurance. And, as many know, this circumstance is quite common, especially for people who are starting their first job or who had insurance through their employer. For those with employer provided coverage, when they quit or lose their job, they are technically uninsured. But they are simply in transition between one insurer through their employer and another.

Advocates of universal care often throw around the 45.7-million figure as if 15 percent of America were permanently uninsured. And that, of course, is a considerable stretch of the data.

Uninsured Americans: a closer look

It can be easy to address "the uninsured" as a single, undifferentiated group. But that is by no means the case. People may be uninsured for different reasons, and if we are to improve America's health system, we need to know more about this perplexing group.

So who are these 45.7 million people? It turns out that the big headline number so often in the news includes a surprisingly wide range of people.

Some, of course, just can't afford to pay for insurance. But others—many, in fact—are uninsured for reasons not directly related to cost, and very likely would not want to be "rescued" by mandatory socialized medicine.

Voluntarily uninsured

Spend just a few minutes with the breakout of the Census Bureau data and some surprising facts about the uninsured population jump out—facts that might change the way you think about the much-discussed American "health care crisis."

How's this for starters? Almost 18 million of the uninsured make more than $50,000 a year. And almost 10 million of them have an income of more than $75,000 a year.[7]

In other words, 38 percent of the U.S. uninsured population earn more than $50,000 per year.

We may be accustomed to thinking of the uninsured as down-and-outs, low-income individuals and families struggling to get by. But the Census Bureau breakout shows that the average uninsured person in the United States makes an above-average income.

How can this be?

Well, for one thing, a great number of financially comfortable young Americans who are not covered by their employer *choose* not to purchase health insurance. Known in the health care trade as the "invincibles" because they're so sure they're healthy and unlikely to get sick, these young singles would rather pocket their monthly insurance premiums than shell out for health care coverage. And, $30 billion by the uninsured was paid for health care out of a total of $86 billion.[8]

Foolish though it may be, this kind of intentional avoidance of health insurance is quite common. According to the Commonwealth Fund, Americans aged 19 to 29 comprise one of the largest and fastest-growing segments of the uninsured population.[9]

And that's just part of the real story of the uninsured. Other factors also cast very large shadows over the big Census Bureau number.

Health Insurance Doesn't Have to Hurt

"Like most young people, I like to believe I'm invincible. Every so often, though, an email shows up in my inbox that reminds me I'm not. Another twentysomething acquaintance has suffered a ski accident, appendectomy, or electric-saw mishap. The worst reports share a line: "he doesn't have health insurance"....Government is the problem, at least when it comes to health insurance. Well-meaning but misguided states such as New Jersey and Massachusetts have priced young people out of the market by keeping laws on the books that force plans to cover everything, take all comers, or treat young and old, healthy and sick, roughly the same.

—Laura Vanderkam, *USA Today*.[10]

Uninsured non-citizens

The 45.7 million "Americans" include large numbers of non-citizens who replied to the Census Bureau survey. In fact, the Census Bureau's breakout shows that more than 10 million of the people considered uninsured by the U.S. government aren't U.S. citizens at all. Some political commentators have estimated that the number is as high as one in four.[11]

It is certainly unfortunate that these individuals have no health insurance (although they can still get free treatment in U.S. emergency rooms), but even a fully nationalized health care system would be unlikely to provide health insurance for them.

Yet the press—the *Boston Globe*, *USA Today*, *New York Times*, and virtually every other major U.S. newspaper—continues to cite this statistic even though it includes a high percentage of non-U.S. citizens. (I must confess, it's such a common statistic that I even reference it multiple times throughout this book.)

Nevertheless, almost 25 percent of those 45.7 million aren't Americans, but merely residents of the United States.

Low-income uninsured

However eye-opening, the above arguments don't counter the fact that many citizens of the United States want health care but can't afford it. Doesn't something need to be done to ensure that poor and lower-income Americans have decent access to affordable, high-quality health care?

In fact, the United States government already offers many in this very group a big hand up. As many as 14 million of the 45.7 million uninsured—poor and low-income Americans—are fully eligible for generous government assistance programs like Medicare, Medicaid, and SCHIP.[12] The problem is, they're just not enrolling in these programs.

"You may think that a poor single mom with three children living in South Central Los Angeles is among the uninsured, but in fact, she is eligible for Medicaid, as are her children. . . . Because Medicaid and children's health programs allow patients to be signed up literally in the [emergency room], these individuals could be covered; they just choose not to do the paperwork," writes Dr. David Gratzer.[13]

As it turns out, a 2008 study by the Georgetown University Health Policy Institute shows that a whopping 70 percent of uninsured children are eligible for either Medicaid, SCHIP, or both programs.[14]

In justifying his national health care plan, Barack Obama often complains that "nearly eight million children" lack health insurance.[15] What he doesn't tell you is that six million of those children are currently uninsured for no reason other than the fact that they have not been enrolled in available programs.

Meanwhile, according to the Urban Institute roughly 27 percent of non-elderly Americans who are eligible for Medicaid simply haven't enrolled, and live their lives without health insurance.[16]

You should keep "failure to enroll" in mind the next time you hear appeals to "expand Medicare to all Americans" like the plan proposed in 2007 by Senators Edward Kennedy (D-MA) and John Dingell (D-MI).[17]

Do we need a mandatory free lunch?

Many point to Medicare, Medicaid, and SCHIP as milestones on the road to government health care. But the easy political rhetoric doesn't even address the issue of people who fall through the cracks of existing programs that supposedly already entitle them to health insurance.

Can we really argue that such people don't have health insurance? Have we reached a state where the government has to force people to show up for a free lunch?

If 14 million eligibles aren't availing themselves of taxpayer-funded coverage, then why should we think that a still bigger government health care bureaucracy will solve the problem?

Who's left?

Okay. So there are supposedly 45.7 million uninsured.

But 18 million earn more than $50,000.

More than 10 million aren't U.S. citizens.

And as many as 14 million qualify for government programs like Medicare, Medicaid, and SCHIP.

Obviously, there's some overlap in these numbers. But the critical question is—who's left over?

Sadly, there are people who really do fall through the cracks. These are the chronically uninsured working poor. They are people who hold down jobs and struggle to support families. They earn less than $50,000 per year, but too much to qualify for government help. And because insurance is so expensive, they simply can't afford it.

There are roughly eight million of these chronically uninsured, and they really do need help.[18] (It should be noted that even though they don't have insurance, they can still get emergency room care for, say, a broken leg, visit a community hospital, or a community clinic. But they aren't covered for routine check-ups and preventative care.)

Any attempt to solve the uninsured problem should focus on this narrow slice of the 45.7-million pie.

Moreover, the key to helping these people isn't to create more government red tape. We have too much of that already. In fact, too much regulation is why health insurance is so expensive in the first place. What these people need is straightforward coverage that they can afford and that will cover catastrophes. That is the purpose of insurance.

In Myth Six, I'll discuss how existing government regulations have driven up costs to the point of absurdity. And in the Solutions chapter of this book, we'll look at some simple ways to fix the problem and lower costs so that even the working poor can easily afford good health coverage.

The myth continues, despite the facts

This chapter begins by quoting Barack Obama's official website: "46 million Americans—including nearly eight million children—lack health insurance with no signs of this trend slowing down."

We've already addressed his first two points regarding "46 million uninsured" and "eight million children." But what about this continuing trend?

When Obama says the trend is not "slowing down," he presumably means that as the U.S. population grows, so too does the number of uninsured.

That's true. But it doesn't tell us much other than the obvious.

Apparently, Obama has overlooked a more interesting—and telling—trend: Over the past 10 years, the situation for low-income uninsured Americans has gotten better, not worse.

According to the Census Bureau's report, the number of households with annual incomes of less than $25,000 who lack health insurance has gone down steadily since 1998.[19]

Surprisingly, the fastest-growing segment of the uninsured is households making *more* than $75,000 a year. For these people, it may be a lack of planning and responsibility, not a lack of access, that is preventing them from being insured.[20]

So the question remains: Is there an uninsured crisis in America today?

The answer—I think—is yes. But it involves dramatically fewer people than is commonly cited.

Myth Four: High Drug Prices Drive Up Health Care Costs

Are excessive drug prices the reason that health care costs are so high today? At first glance, it definitely seems that way.

In 2007, the United States spent $286.5 billion on prescription drugs.[1] That's a whopping figure. To put it into perspective, it's more than the entire GDP of Ireland.[2] Or almost $2,600 per household.[3]

That same year, Pfizer, the world's largest drug company, had revenues totaling nearly $50 billion.[4]

These aren't pie-in-the-sky numbers. They directly affect real patients. Lipitor, Pfizer's bestselling drug, retails for about $100 for a month's supply.[5] So most people who take the daily cholesterol-lowering pill spend around $1,200 annually just to fill their prescription. That's money they could have spent taking their kids to the movies, or going on vacation.

And Lipitor isn't even that expensive. In fact, compared to some drugs, it's a bargain. Avastin, the cutting-edge biologic drug manufactured by Genentech for treating colon, lung, and breast cancer, costs as much as $100,000 for a year's supply.[6] That's more than double what the median American household earns in a year.[7]

Meanwhile, prescription drugs are taking up a greater portion of health care spending than ever before. Whereas drug spending hovered between 5 and 8 percent of overall health care expenditures from the mid-1970s until about 10 years ago, it has steadily climbed past the 10-percent mark in recent years.[8]

Critics often point to these facts as proof that drugs are driving up the nation's health care costs. And it's easy to think they're right . . . if you just look at a few isolated statistics.

But they're completely wrong.

There's an old story about a frog who lives at the bottom of a well. One day, he looks up and sees a tiny circle of sky above him. "Ah," he says to himself, "now I've seen the world."

The argument that drug prices are driving up health care costs is as disconnected from reality as that frog at the bottom of the well.

In reality, prescription drugs reduce medical spending.

How? By obviating the need for prolonged hospital stays, surgery, and other expensive procedures like anesthesia.

It's time to climb out of the well and cast some sunlight on this pervasive myth.

Choice in Medicine

When I spoke at the Innovation '08 Conference in San Diego, a conference for CEOs, I was approached after my speech by a doctor who thought the Veterans Administration system for providing care for America's vets and their families should be the model for the country. Of course I didn't agree and I mentioned that, for example, drugs like Lipitor, a new and innovative drug that effectively brings down cholesterol, are not on the list of drugs available to vets. The doctor countered that this was a good thing—because Lipitor is expensive and is no different than the cheaper drugs on the market. I replied that the critical point is that it *works for others* where some of the older, cheaper drugs do not and that these drugs should be available for all so that vets in consultation with their doctors can decide what works best for them.

The elephant in the emergency room

Any discussion of health care costs needs to start with chronic diseases. They are the elephant in the emergency room.

Chronic diseases—conditions like diabetes, cancer in remission, heart disease, HIV, obesity, and arthritis—are far and away the biggest drain on America's health care system. They've led to a massive increase in health care costs in recent decades.

Today, caring for people with chronic diseases accounts for about 85 percent of all U.S. health care spending.[9]

So, clearly, one of the most effective ways to lower overall health care costs is to control chronic disease.[10] And drugs have proven to be one of the most effective—and inexpensive—ways to do just that. They have also allowed many people with these diseases to lead longer and more normal lives.

We're older and fatter

Today, about six in 10 Americans have at least one chronic disease.[11] There are several reasons behind this growing problem. But for the most part, it's the result of an aging—and expanding—population. Simply put, Americans are older and fatter than we used to be.

Just how blubbery are we?

Two in three American adults are overweight.[12] One in three is obese.[13] But, is it the responsibility of government to get us to reduce or is it our responsibility? I believe it is ours.

Just how old are we?

About one in every eight Americans is now over 65. By 2030, the number of senior citizens will explode to one in five Americans.[14]

These statistics help explain why chronic diseases are more prevalent than ever before. At the simplest level, older people are more vulnerable.

Hospital admissions and physician visits

Between 1994 and 2004, the prevalence of diabetes doubled.[15] High blood pressure is also on the rise. In 1994, about one in four American adults had high blood pressure. Today, it's one in three.[16] Heart disease now kills one person every 34 seconds.[17]

According to a study by Gerard Anderson, a professor of health policy and management at Johns Hopkins, people with chronic conditions account for 82 percent of hospital admissions and 79 percent of all physician visits.[18]

According to the same study, people with two chronic diseases cost the health care system about five times more than those with no conditions. And they're four times as likely to be hospitalized.[19]

This makes sense. Untreated diabetes can lead to nerve disease, heart failure, blindness, kidney failure, and limb amputation.[20] Untreated heart disease can lead to stroke, heart attack, and death.

Drugs have proven able to curtail the costs—both physical and financial—of these conditions.

Lipitor is cheaper than heart surgery

Between 1999 and 2006, researchers tracked nearly 45,000 heart patients in 14 countries. The results, published in the *Journal of the American Medical Association*, showed that the rate of death from heart attacks dropped by nearly half during that time. The main reason: increased use of cholesterol-lowering drugs, blood thinners, stents, and angioplasties.[21]

The study also found that from 1999–2005, the proportion of patients who developed congestive heart failure after a heart attack dropped from 19.5 percent to 11 percent.[22]

This medical progress has had a major impact on health care expenditures.

A 2005 study published in *Medical Care* found that every additional dollar spent on drugs for blood pressure, cholesterol, and diabetes shaves $4.00 to $7.00 off other medical spending.[23] Similarly, a recent paper from the National Bureau of Economic Research (NBER) found that Medicare ultimately saves $2.06 for every dollar it spends on medicines.[24]

In other words, drugs save America's health care system a fortune. This makes sense. A daily dosage of Lipitor is cheaper than emergency heart surgery.

Why do drugs cost so much?

Drugs may lower overall health care costs. But that doesn't mean they're cheap.

They're not.

Anyone who has ever had to pay for drugs out of pocket knows that they can be extremely expensive.

So the big question is—why do drugs cost so much?

Some critics argue that drugs are massively overpriced because drug makers are especially greedy. But this is a facile argument that defies common sense—unless, of course, you believe that people who spend their lives developing life-saving medical cures are just naturally more greedy than lawyers, pilots, engineers, politicians, journalists, and virtually any other profession that comes to mind.

In fact, there's a very simple explanation for the high price of prescription drugs: they cost a lot to develop. One reason is that most drugs are complete failures that never make it to the pharmacy shelf. They also fail because harmful side effects are identified during clinical trials or by the FDA which tests for safety and efficacy.

So when a company finally invents a successful drug, it needs to recoup a lot more than the money spent developing the winner. If that company is to stay in business, it also needs to recoup all the money that was spent developing the losers.

And in the world of inventing medical cures, there are a lot of losers.

Tough odds

Inventing new medicines is fraught with risk. For every 5,000 to 10,000 compounds tested, only five will make it to clinical trials. And only one will successfully make it through FDA review and to the market.[25] That's why it takes, on average, 10 to 15 years from the time a new chemical compound is discovered to the time the FDA grants approval.[26]

Needless to say, it's enormously expensive to navigate a drug through the approval process and onto the pharmacy shelf. According to a study from the Tufts University Center for the Study of Drug Development, it takes about $1.3 billion to bring a single new drug to market.[27] And only two in 10 approved drugs earn enough to cover the cost of research and development.[28]

These are tough odds, and yet investors keep putting their money into biotech startups and pharmaceutical research firms.

The reality is that a drug firm's research dollars come from investors. If investors don't stand a good chance of making money, they'll put their money in an industry that can better guarantee a return on investment.

Enormous rewards

Yes, the process of developing medical drugs is incredibly expensive, time-consuming, and risky. But investors continue to fund more research despite the fact that there will be many failures. Why? Because the rewards are so enormous.

The benefits can be measured not just in dollars—but also in human lives saved.

Of the nearly 350 new medicines approved by the FDA in the last decade, we've seen new treatments for strokes, heart disease, diabetes, cystic fibrosis, and cancer.[29]

In December 2007, the Centers for Disease Control and Prevention (CDC) reported that the average cholesterol level in Americans over 20 had finally reached an ideal range—falling below 200 mg/dL for the first time in 50 years. This was a major blow against heart disease—and it was largely due to the use of cholesterol-lowering drugs.[30]

In 2006, U.S. life expectancy hit a record high, hitting 80.7 years for women and 75.4 years for men.[31]

Between 1971 and 2003, the number of cancer medications tripled.[32] Today, the United States leads the world in treating cancer. According to a 2008 study published in *The Lancet Oncology*, the renowned British medical journal, Americans have a better survival rate for 13 of the 16 most prominent cancers when compared to their European and Canadian counterparts.[33]

Currently, there are more than 2,700 new drugs either undergoing FDA review or in clinical trials for almost 5,000 different conditions.[34] Of course, many of these medicines will never make it to patients. But these drugs offer hope to the countless individuals who suffer from cancer, Alzheimer's, and other painful and life-threatening diseases.

Oil doesn't hold a candle to electricity

Drugs are expensive. And the nation is spending more money on them than ever before. Nevertheless, drug prices are steadily dropping.

Confused? It may sound contradictory, but it actually makes perfect sense.

Think about the history of artificial light. Until Thomas Edison invented the incandescent light bulb in the late nineteenth century, people spent money on wood, oil, and candles to light their homes. One could safely say that electricity accounted for zero percent of their artificial-light expenditures.

Suddenly, with the advent of the light bulb in the 1880s, electricity started to take over. People gradually stopped lighting their homes with oil, wood, and candles—and started spending money on electricity. Eventually, electricity accounted for nearly 100 percent of all artificial-light expenditures.

Electricity spending absolutely soared. And the reason was obvious—oil doesn't hold a candle to electricity.

Now imagine if the nation had fretted that electricity prices were rising too quickly in the 1890s. What if candle-makers had been able to plant newspaper articles complaining that spending on electricity was rising too quickly?

What if the oil-lamp industry had persuaded politicians that electricity accounted for too high a percentage of overall light expenditures? And what if those politicians then passed laws punishing light-bulb makers for being greedy?

In short, if electricity had faced the political and media attack that we're witnessing today against drugs, we'd still be living in the dark—literally.[35]

Below the rate of inflation

Just as electricity transformed the artificial-light industry, drugs have caused a similar sea change in the health care industry. Even though overall drug spending is up, drug prices themselves have not increased. In fact, they've fallen.

In September 2007, the U.S. Department of Labor reported that the annual inflation rate for drug prices was at its lowest in the three decades since it began tracking such numbers. The annual inflation rate for pharmaceuticals was 1 percent, well below the rate of overall inflation. Principally, this was the result of increased use of generic drugs.[36]

The rise of generics—and falling prices

Generic drugs are chemically identical to their brand-name counterparts,[37] and they're more popular than ever. In 2007, generics accounted for 65 percent of all prescriptions filled in U.S. pharmacies.[38] And that percentage is expected to increase as the patents on a host of blockbuster drugs will soon expire.[39]

Meanwhile, over the past few years, the price of generics has plummeted. Between 2003 and 2007, according to a recent report from AARP's Public Policy Institute, the prices for 125 generic drugs popular among older Americans dropped by 16.5 percent. Over that same time frame, general inflation rose 16.5 percent.[40]

The reason for this price drop? Free-market competition.

Competition brings free drugs

In the fall of 2006, Wal-Mart began offering a host of generic prescriptions for just $4 a month. Almost immediately, other retailers—including Wegmans, BJs, and Target—announced similar plans.

Then, in August 2007, Publix, a grocery store chain in the southeastern United States, announced something even more spectacular: It would offer seven commonly-used antibiotics for free to get consumers into its stores.[41]

It was an incredible display of the amazing benefits of a free market. Not only did this price competition result in cheaper medicine—it actually led to free drugs.

A dangerous myth

The widespread belief that drugs are responsible for high health care costs is not a harmless myth. It has led to a surreal situation in which politicians are attempting to punish the very industry that is driving overall prices down.

A number of politicians, including members of Congress, are now pushing to impose price controls—along with other innovation-stifling regulations—on the pharmaceutical industry. If they succeed, it would have a disastrous, dampening effect on the invention of new medical cures.

If pharmaceutical manufacturers are forced to sell drugs at below-market prices, they will simply become a less attractive investment opportunity. As a result, investors will stop funding the research that creates new cures. Life-saving breakthroughs will be lost.[42] And ironically, overall health care costs will rise as more people wind up in the emergency room for their medical treatment.

It may seem counterintuitive, but expensive breakthrough drugs usually save money. The research bears it out. Columbia University professor Frank Lichtenberg recently published a paper with the National Bureau of Economic Research—and the results were extraordinary.

According to Lichtenberg, switching from older, cheaper medicines to newer, pricier ones reduced non-drug health care expenses by more than seven times as much as it raised drug spending.[43]

In short, those who complain about high drug prices are penny wise and pound foolish. To a frog at the bottom of a well, a light bulb might seem expensive. But it's a lot cheaper—and more efficient—than a year's worth of candles.

Myth Five: Importing Drugs Would Reduce Health Care Costs

Perhaps the most popular solution for lowering overall health care costs today is to legalize the importation of drugs from abroad.

In the 2008 presidential campaign, the candidates of both parties—John McCain and Barack Obama—maintained that Americans should be allowed to fill their prescriptions from foreign pharmacies. But the scares over the safety of imported drugs from other countries caused both candidates to question this proposal. They both, however, supported making it easier and faster to get generics and follow-on biologics.

It's not surprising that Democrats and Republicans have supported this issue. Voters overwhelmingly support importation—or about eight out of 10 people, according to one *Wall Street Journal*/Harris Interactive poll.[1]

It's easy to see why drug importation is so popular. Brand-name drugs are often cheaper overseas. In Canada, prices can be as much as 70 percent lower than in the United States.[2]

Many Americans would love to take advantage of these lower prices. But they can't because federal law restricts the availability of imported pharmaceuticals, except under very specific circumstances.

This seems unnecessary. Wouldn't it make more sense just to open up the floodgates and let Americans purchase medicine over the Internet from virtually any country around the globe—and theoretically save a significant amount of money? Or better yet, why not let big U.S. pharmacies like CVS buy foreign drugs in bulk? Wouldn't that lower prices for everybody?

At first glance, importation appears to be an elegant and easy solution to rising health care costs. Removing the legal dam would flood the U.S. market with cheap foreign pills, significantly reducing drug spending without sacrificing health care quality.

Or at least it seems that way.

Unfortunately, things aren't always as they seem—and a closer look at the facts reveals that the promise of importation falls dangerously short of the reality.

When it comes to legislative solutions, it's often said that the devil is in the details. Perhaps nowhere is this truer than in the policy debate over drug importation.

Why are some drugs cheaper abroad?

Before we tackle the problems of legalizing importation, we must first understand why brand-name drugs made by U.S. companies are sometimes cheaper abroad.

The reason is simple: The governments of most foreign countries have imposed price controls on prescription drugs. They do this in order to keep costs low so that they're able to sustain their government health care systems.

In Canada, for example, an agency called the Patented Medicine Prices Review Board ensures that drug prices are not excessive. The board strictly monitors the prices at which manufacturers may sell drugs to wholesalers and pharmacies, and at which pharmacies may sell to the public.

To save funds, Canadian health officials routinely delay the approval of new and more expensive drugs. And even after a drug is approved and a price set, the provincial governments decide whether to put it on the formularies.

As a result it takes considerable time for new and more expensive medications to make it into the medicine chests of Canadians. Some never do. One hundred new drugs were launched in the United States from 1997 through 1999. Only 43 made it to market in Canada in that same period. Canadians are still waiting for many life-saving drugs that are currently available in the United States.[3] Cancer and AIDS drugs are important examples. In fact, the U.S. has taken the lead worldwide in innovative performance and as a first-launch location for new drug introductions.[4]

Advanced drugs aren't available

I'm originally Canadian, so I've seen how this works up close and personal. In 2003, my uncle was diagnosed with non-Hodgkin's lymphoma. If he'd lived in America, the miracle drug Rituxan might have saved him. But Rituxan wasn't approved for use in Canada, and he lost his battle with cancer.

A couple of years ago, I received an email from a woman in Ontario who had heard my uncle's story. Her reason for writing? She wanted to let me know that Rituxan still wasn't available— so she was about to embark on a trip to Michigan for the drug.

That's the grim reality of price controls—they lead to rationing. Similar tragedies have played out over and over again in Britain, France, Italy, and virtually every other country that imposes price controls on drugs.

That's why even as Americans are flocking to the Internet to buy inexpensive drugs from abroad, Canadians and Europeans have for years been coming to the United States, desperately seeking critical medicines that they can't obtain in their own countries. And they're willing to pay top-dollar for these drugs out of their own pockets.

A few years ago, a friend of mine in New Brunswick, who suffers from type 2 diabetes, learned that Glucophage XR—an oral blood-sugar-control medication made by U.S. manufacturer Bristol-Myers Squibb—would be the most effective drug for him. But it wasn't available in New Brunswick. So he had to travel to Bangor, Maine, about four and a half hours' drive away, to get it.

So, yes, some drugs are, in fact, cheaper abroad because governments have imposed price controls. But many of the most cutting-edge drugs aren't available at all in other countries.

Not always cheaper

But what about the drugs that are available abroad? Aren't they less expensive?

Not necessarily. While it's true that brand-name drugs are usually cheaper, the majority of drugs are actually more expensive abroad. That's because most drugs consumed in the United States are generics—i.e., copies of brand-name drugs that are no longer under patent protection.

Generics accounted for 65 percent of the U.S. drug market in 2007, and they're dramatically cheaper in the United States than anywhere else in the world. The reason generics are so cheap in the United States is that, unlike in Europe and Canada, there's a flourishing free market here, and competition drives prices down.

That's why you can walk into a Wal-Mart or a Target today and buy $4 generics. You can't do that in France, Britain, or Canada.

A narrow category

So when people say, "drugs are cheaper in other countries," they're making an enormous generalization. What they really should say is that certain brand-name drugs are cheaper. They're not referring to generics. And they're not referring to all the cutting-edge drugs that aren't available in other countries.

Instead, they're referring to a very narrow category—brand-name drugs that have been approved and price-controlled by foreign governments. These price-controlled drugs are generally about 50 percent cheaper in Europe and Canada.

Shouldering the burden

Currently, the United States produces the vast majority of the world's cutting-edge drugs precisely because the free market still plays a role here. It's no surprise that America spends four times as much per year as the United Kingdom, and a whopping 17 times as much as Canada, to research and develop new drugs.

Meanwhile, as we've seen, it takes about $1.3 billion to bring a new drug to market.[5] By contrast, the cost of producing, packaging, and distributing pills is miniscule. The first pill costs more than a billion dollars to produce; the second pill is gumball cheap.

Advocates of importation like to pretend R&D costs don't exist—as if ground-breaking pills were simply Tic-Tacs. But they're not. And if companies cannot recoup and ultimately profit from their investments, they will have no incentive to continue developing new life-saving drugs.

The problem is that someone has to pay for that first pill. Someone has to foot the massive bill for research and development. Right now, the American consumer is shouldering this burden. I agree that's not fair. But the answer is not to destroy our own pharmaceutical industry. Rather, our government needs to pressure foreign countries to remove price controls and share the cost.

Why we put up with it

No doubt, many readers are wondering: If Americans are getting such a raw deal from foreign countries like Canada, why do U.S. companies continue to sell them drugs at discount prices?

The answer is simple—patent theft. Again, Canada is a perfect example. The Canadian Government has promised that if U.S. companies refuse to sell drugs to Canada, it will retaliate by allowing generic companies to steal American patents and reproduce the drugs at a lower price.

In fact, by threatening to violate patents, the Canadian government routinely pressures American companies into selling at below-market rates. It's theft—plain and simple.

Thus, there's another reason U.S. drug companies are willing to sell at a discount to foreign countries. They're able to recoup their R&D costs from U.S. consumers, who pay more than their fair share and effectively subsidize consumers in other countries. So long as the U.S. market remains segmented from foreign price-controlled markets, drug companies don't lose money by stamping out the additional pills for Canadians and Europeans.

Think of an airline that has a plane that's not fully booked. Once enough passengers have bought tickets to cover the cost of the flight, the airline can then sell the extra seats at below-market prices and still make money. American drug consumers are like the airline passengers who pay full freight so the flight can actually take off. To put it bluntly, the rest of the world is free-riding.

Free-riding works so long as the overall market is profitable. But if everyone tries to free-ride, then the system breaks down.

For example, if U.S. pharmaceutical corporations see their drugs returning *en masse* to the United States at below-market prices, they will respond by refusing to sell drugs to overseas distributors.

If more Americans use the Internet to buy drugs illegally from abroad, U.S. companies should respond by limiting their shipments. Some U.S. companies are boycotting mail-order pharmacies. Our government should stand behind them. Rather than rewarding foreign governments for blackmailing American companies, our politicians should be pressuring other countries to honor U.S. patents and pay their fare share of R&D costs.

The devil is in the details

Unfortunately, our politicians are doing just the opposite. They're actually encouraging their fellow politicians to support and impose price controls on our companies.

U.S. lawmakers recognize that importation alone wouldn't actually lower costs. If there were a true global free market in drugs, then U.S. drug makers would respond by raising prices on foreign distributors—and prices would equalize across national markets.

In that scenario, here's what would happen. Prices would drop slightly in the United States, while rising significantly for foreign consumers. That's because the U.S. is the biggest market by a long shot.

Think of a dam separating a low lake from an ocean. If the dam breaks, and the water level equalizes, the ocean's level doesn't drop much. But the lake's water level rises dramatically. That's what happens when markets are desegregated. The bigger markets experience less change.

For U.S. policymakers who are promising cheap drugs, simply desegregating the markets though importation wouldn't achieve much cost savings.

What these pro-importation politicians really want to do is to force U.S. prices down dramatically. To do that, they need to prevent U.S. companies from equalizing prices.

If you look carefully at almost all the importation legislation that has been floating through the halls of Congress—and there's a lot of it—there's almost always a "forced sale" provision that would require American companies to sell drugs to foreign exporters at rates determined by foreign governments.

Such legislation would essentially impose foreign price-controls on U.S. companies. It would have almost exactly the same effect as if our government imposed price controls directly.

Senator Byron Dorgan (D-ND) has been one of the most ardent sponsors of "forced sale" importation. His legislation would force America's drug industry to do business with a metaphorical gun to its head.

No matter the price or quantity demanded by foreign governments, American businesses would be required by law to sell. They would also be required to sell to foreign drug resellers, who would then be able to export their countries' price controls to the United States. Such legislation is an affront to all American businesses, a violation of essential patent rights, and a threat to free trade.

Bully bargaining

It's not deal-making—it's bully bargaining.

Imagine, for example, if you could walk into Best Buy and set your own low price for a 60-inch plasma television. This might sound great at first. But it wouldn't take long before the store, no longer able to ensure the stream of revenue it needed, would have to drastically reduce its offerings—or possibly even shut down entirely.

Free trade and fair business dealings require consent from both parties; any law requiring forced sale would undermine the underlying principles of both.

U.S. pharmaceutical companies are no different from Best Buy—
or even Dreyer's. Every business must mark up its products to turn
a profit. If politicians single out drug companies and deny them
a return on their investments, those companies will simply stop
investing in the development of new drugs. One can't help wondering whether U.S. lawmakers want to turn the pharmaceutical
industry into a regulated public utility.

Stifling innovation

Pharmaceuticals are already a risky investment. As we showed earlier in the Tufts study, the average drug costs $1.3 billion to bring to
market, and takes nearly a decade in research and development.[6]

Investors are willing to take that chance precisely because the
rewards of developing a cure for non-Hodgkins lymphoma, AIDS,
or diabetes are considerable. If price controls are imposed, the profit
incentive would be removed. Investment dollars would dry up. And
the miracle cures that mark America's drug industry would vanish.

That's exactly what's happening in price-controlled countries:
Venture capitalists invest 15 times more in American biotech
companies than in European ones.[7]

Less investment means fewer breakthrough medicines. The Department of Health and Human Services estimates that importation
could cause four to 18 fewer drugs to be developed per decade.[8]

Americans aren't the only ones who would lose out from a ham-
strung pharmaceutical industry. U.S. firms are responsible for
almost 90 percent of new drugs worldwide.[9] An indigent African
farmer's anti-malarial drug cocktail, a French diplomat's heart
medication, an Italian prime minister's pacemaker, a Japanese

businessman's antidepressants—all were probably invented by an American pharmaceutical or medical device firm.

Illusory cost savings

Making matters even worse, importation by forced-sale wouldn't even save much money for U.S. consumers. A 2003 study from the London School of Economics that looked at a similar policy in the European Union found that such rules don't lead to lower prices at the drugstore.[10] Instead, only the middlemen—those foreign pharmacies that purchase the drugs in bulk and resell them—would benefit.

The cost savings promised by the pro-importation crowd are mostly illusory. The Congressional Budget Office (CBO) estimates that foreign drug importation would only reduce national drug expenditure by one percent over the next decade. Researchers noted that Canadian importation would lead to a "negligible reduction in drug spending."[11]

Tried and failed

In fact, drug importation has already been tried—and it has failed miserably, over and over again. A number of states have shirked federal law and established their own local drug importation programs. Not one has been popular.

Take Illinois. In 2004, Governor Rod Blagojevich implemented the "I-SaveRx" program which, in conjunction with neighboring Wisconsin, allowed state residents to buy meds from Canadian pharmacies.

The program cost $1 million in taxpayer dollars, requiring services from 500 public employees and two dozen state agencies. The day Blagojevish introduced the bill establishing I-SaveRx, he boldly declared:

The nearly 13 million people who live in Illinois and the more than five million people who live in Wisconsin will have the opportunity to save hundreds—and in some cases even thousands—of dollars each year on the high cost of their medicine.

After 19 months of operation, only 3,689 Illinois residents had used the I-SaveRx program. That's just 0.02 percent of the state population.[12]

It's a similar story with other importation programs. The one in Missouri has attracted all of 460 customers; Wisconsin 321; Kansas 267; and Vermont 217. In 2004, the city council of Portland, Maine instituted a Canadian import program for city employees and their families. By 2007, it had only 350 participants.[13]

The truth about importation

Unfortunately, despite all these failures at the state level, federal politicians continue to push for importation. If they're successful, it would be a health care disaster for not only Americans but individuals worldwide.

When politicians say we should legalize importation, they're not being honest. What they really should say is that they want to impose foreign price controls on U.S. drug companies, while driving away the investors who fund the creation of new medical cures that allow us to live longer and healthier lives.

The irony is that their importation scheme wouldn't even save money for U.S. consumers.

Myth Six: Universal Coverage Can Be Achieved by Forcing Everyone to Buy Insurance

From state governors to presidential candidates, U.S. politicians routinely claim that virtually all our health care problems would be solved if only every man, woman, and child were covered by health insurance.

How do they suggest we achieve this utopian goal? Simple: Pass a law that requires everyone to buy coverage. Many politicians in Congress are now pushing for exactly that—a law that would supposedly end the problem of the uninsured by *requiring* all Americans to have health insurance.

Unfortunately it's not that easy.

Mark Twain once quipped, "Facts are stubborn things." Well, people are, too.

If waving a congressional wand and saying "Make it so," solved problems, we'd have ended war, poverty, and homelessness long ago. Take car insurance. People are required to have it. But many find ways around the rules, especially when they would have to spend their own money.

Although car insurance is mandatory in all but two states[1], nearly 15 percent of drivers are still out on the roads uninsured.[2] Yet, despite what we know about economics and human nature, the mandate myth has become a common refrain in the health care reform debate today.

Who are these health care scofflaws?

To believe that universal health care coverage can be achieved through a legal mandate is to misunderstand how people react to do-good laws and why. The academics, policy experts, media voices, and employers cheering for mandates assume that uninsured Americans either are just too lazy to purchase health insurance, or don't have the money to pay for it.

That makes it easy to fix, so the argument goes. If it's illegal *not* to purchase insurance, even the lazy folks will pony up. And for those who can't afford it—presto!—a government subsidy will make insurance affordable. In other words, if people are threatened with a buck-up-or-pay-up fine, and/or given the chance to purchase a policy at a mere fraction of their monthly wages, they'll jump through the hoop and become responsible citizens.[3]

That might make sense in theory. But in reality, Americans are both stubborn, and smart. Most of those who do not purchase health insurance make that choice not because they don't have the resources or because they're lazy, but because they've done the math and don't want to spend their money on expensive insurance policies that don't fit their individual or family needs.

In the United States today, as we discussed in Myth Three, there are around 46 million people[4] with no health insurance—some 15 percent of the population. Who are those 46 million?

Many think they're our poorest, oldest, or youngest citizens. But as we also discussed in Myth Three, that's not the case at all. For the most part, those three groups are already covered by government health programs. Medicaid covers many of the poor and disabled. Medicare covers the old. And the State Children's Health Insurance Plan (SCHIP) covers the young who fall through the gaps.

So who's hiding?

Two groups: 1) those who earn too much money to qualify for Medicaid, but not enough to afford individual health insurance; and 2) those who can afford insurance, but simply choose not to purchase coverage.

As it turns out, the bulk of the uninsured (not counting people who qualify for, but don't enroll in, Medicaid, Medicare, or SCHIP) fall into the second group. These are people who have chosen not to buy insurance for entirely rational reasons.

People won't pay for what they don't use

Take a typical healthy 24-year-old woman who has just entered the workforce but whose employer does not provide health care coverage. She might very well decide that $300 a month for health insurance—a typical rate for a single person—isn't worth it for the few medical services she needs.

It would be a terrific waste of money for her to pay nearly $4,000 per year so that she can be covered for regular doctor visits, when she rarely goes to the doctor in the first place.

She's smart enough to realize she should have a so-called "cata-strophic" policy, which comes with a low premium, and has a high deductible, but would protect her from the worst of the worst medical problems.

But guess what? Such a sensible policy is very difficult—if not impossible—to find. Thanks to state-level laws and regula-tions telling insurers they can't tailor policies for the young and healthy, such policies are unavailable in many U.S. markets. It's all or nothing for our young woman.

And faced with the choice between a pricey policy—covering everything including, say, testicular cancer—or no policy at all, it's no surprise that she chooses to forego health insurance entirely. Perhaps she chooses to put the money into savings or textbooks instead, or into nights on the town. The point is, it's her choice, not the government's.

What mandate laws do is turn around and tell that healthy young person that she *has to pay her fair share* and buy health insurance, like it or not. A mandate is really a stealth form of taxation. At the most basic level, mandates deprive people of the freedom to do as they choose with their money.

Not surprisingly, those people balk when they're ordered to get in line at the health insurance window and pay up. That's exactly what happened in Massachusetts, when the state passed a law in April 2006 mandating insurance coverage either through an individual policy or lose their personal income tax deduction, or by forcing employers to provide it.

People balked. There were still 168,000 adults who remained without health insurance at the end of 2007. More than half of them—97,000—remained uninsured even though they were per-fectly able to afford a policy, according to the state Department of Revenue, which combed through their tax returns.[5]

Apparently, these scofflaws just didn't want to pay for an expen-sive insurance plan they didn't need—even if it were the law.

So what if it's bad for business?

Mandates on businesses depress economic growth.

Across the country, various states are experimenting with man-date laws. From Hawaii to Maine, today's mandate proposals are usually two-pronged:

The first prong forces individuals who aren't covered by their employer or a subsidized program to purchase insurance on their own. The second prong forces employers—usually ones above a certain size—to provide health insurance to their workers or pay a percentage of payroll into a state-sponsored fund. This is referred to as "pay or play." Many businesses these days do provide health insurance to their employees, both as a worker incentive and because they get tax breaks for doing so. But health insurance is a major expense, and companies that don't provide it usually have chosen not to because they can't afford to absorb such a huge expense into their overhead.

The Massachusetts mandate requires companies with 11 or more full-time employees to cover their workers or face a fine of $295. That could put many a struggling company out of business, and all their employees out of work. Such a mandate also discour-ages new businesses from opening up. And it discourages existing businesses from expanding. The state of Massachusetts, it seems, would rather subsidize unemployment than let people earn a wage that doesn't come with health care attached.

The facts from Massachusetts

A more detailed look at the Bay State's experience shows us the perils and pitfalls of health insurance mandates.

Massachusetts' 2006 law passed with strong backing from Republican then-governor Mitt Romney, whose oft-proclaimed goal was to achieve statewide universal health insurance coverage.

His reform was premised on the idea that universal coverage was a moral imperative. It took a bipartisan effort to pass: Senator Edward Kennedy (D–MA) helped persuade the state's Democratic legislators, while Romney handled the business community.[6]

Massachusetts had learned lessons from other state-level attempts to get more people covered by health insurance. Maine, for example, had passed its Dirigo Health Reform Act in 2003, which promised to bring coverage to 30,000 of the state's uninsured immediately, and ramp up to 140,000 Mainers by 2005.

Today, though, enrollment in Maine remains at only 25 percent of projections. The Dirigo scheme required users to ante up a monthly premium, and some Mainers simply didn't want to pay. They tended to be healthy folks who used the system only occasionally and who perhaps had few assets to protect. Some indeed jumped at the chance to get cut-rate insurance. But unfortunately they tended to be older, less healthy, and, well, heavy users of the system.[7]

In insurance, that's called negative or adverse selection and it can send costs through the roof and projections out the window because it results in a smaller pool of healthy premium payers supporting a higher number of unhealthy payers. Only the sick get a good deal.

The Maine experience showed Massachusetts policymakers that you need sticks as well as carrots to bring the population to heel in matters of insurance.

The carrots were establishing more aggressive taxpayer-subsidies for insurance costs and allowing the uninsured to use pre-tax dollars to purchase individual plans. The sticks: stiff fines for both individuals and employers who failed to "take advantage" of the opportunity to buy in.[8]

The number of people enrolled in Massachusetts health care plans did in fact increase. Before enactment of the law in April 2006, the state's uninsured numbered between 550,000 and 715,000— or 8.6 to 11.2 percent of the population of 6.4 million. By the summer of 2008, about 350,000 of the previously uninsured had enrolled.[9] About half, or 175,000, chose Commonwealth Care, a heavily subsidized or free insurance program for adults who earn no more than three times the federal poverty level, but who don't have access to other government-sponsored programs or to employer insurance.[10]

The bill to taxpayers, though, has mounted far faster than the policymakers predicted. Commonwealth Care cost the state $133 million in fiscal year 2007, about $647 million in 2008, and is estimated to cost $869 million in fiscal year 2009[11]—and could reach $1.1 billion, according to Governor Deval Patrick.[12]

Meanwhile, when the plan was first introduced, then-Governor Mitt Romney predicted that it would cost only $125 million a year.[13]

Now that's a cost overrun that should make even a politician blush.

And there's more to this particular mandate story. State projections of fines to be collected from companies that failed to cover employees' health insurance were radically off base. They were supposed to total $50 million a year and be used to offset the costs of the subsidies. Instead of $50 million, fines were projected to bring in just $6.7 million in 2008.[14]

That's a massive misjudgment. Imagine if, say, a Nasdaq-listed company assured shareholders that it was on track to earn $50 million for the year and then earned only $6.7 million. Shareholders would be outraged. There would probably be a lot of firings. Unfortunately, there are no shareholders to hold the Massachusetts government accountable. So the cost overruns and outlandish projections continue to this day.

Not so universal after all

As bureaucrats struggle to keep costs down, has the Massachusetts program at least achieved the goal of universal coverage? The evidence points to a resounding no.

Obviously, with enough encouragement, people will take advantage of heavily subsidized or free services. In Massachusetts, 175,000 residents signed up for subsidized Commonwealth Care policies. And the state also reported a rise in new Medicaid cardholders—about 87,000.[15]

But the plan didn't fare so well when people had to purchase full-ticket insurance. Enrollments in Commonwealth Choice, through which the government offers full-price, unsubsidized policies, totaled only 18,122 as of May 1, 2008.[16]

By the summer of 2008, about 5 percent of the state's population remained uninsured.[17] The state threw up its hands and allowed many of them to remain so. Massachusetts offered exemptions for 20 percent of its citizens[18] who earn too much to qualify for the subsidized programs, but not enough to afford the cost of insurance on the private market.[19]

Exploding bureaucracy

Call them the insurance police.

As soon as you start telling people they have to spend money they don't want to spend on something they don't want, somebody is going to have to make sure they actually do it. That's why individual mandates inevitably lead to new enforcement bureaucracies.

In Massachusetts, the state Department of Revenue went over 2007 tax returns to figure out how many adults remained without health insurance (168,000), and how many of them, in the Department's view, were "able to afford" insurance (97,000).[20] Penalties were issued, appeals heard, exemptions granted. In 2007, the penalty was $219. In 2008, it increases to $912.[21]

Who do you think managed this whole process? A brand-new bureaucracy and the Commonwealth Connector, where individuals were supposed to be able to find affordable insurance plans. And don't even ask about the costs.

Mandates don't control rising prices

Forcing people to buy health insurance whether they like it or not is problematic enough. A bigger issue, though, is that mandates ignore what's really driving up health care costs.

Health insurance gets more expensive, in part, because the prices of the services it covers are rising. Cutting-edge medicines and technologies tend to be high-priced when they arrive on the market, and gradually get cheaper as they become more common and widely available, or, in the case of drugs, when their patents expire.

Short of putting a stop to groundbreaking research, there's not all that much policymakers can do about that side of the cost conundrum unless we get to the point of across-the-board price controls which, as any economist will tell you, brings rationing and black markets.

But there are two additional reasons health insurance is expensive. One is that the 60 percent of Americans who get their insurance tax-free through their employer are insulated from the true cost of health care and hence, use more of it and second, because mandated coverage requirements severely limit the market's ability to develop and offer inexpensive plans that meet buyers' needs.[22]

When more coverage equals less coverage

Politicians love to show their sympathy and concern by increasing benefits.

State governments continue to pass what are called benefit mandates, laws requiring health plans to pay for, or at least offer, specified treatments or types of providers. For example, a mandate may require a health plan to cover treatment for alcoholism, or chiropractic services.

In 1979 there were *only* 252 mandate laws in force—an average of five per state.[23] By 2007, according to the Council for Affordable

Health Insurance, there were *1,901* such mandates, which works out to an average of 38 mandates per state.[24]

Benefit mandates introduced since 2000 include hearing aids, hormone replacement therapy, and reimbursement for clinical trial participation.[25] Many mandates—like massage therapy, breast reduction, and hair prosthesis—are hardly critical components of a good health insurance policy. They exist because special-interest groups—say, chiropractors—have lobbied state lawmakers to require all insurance policies to cover their particular service.

The result is that costs are driven up for everybody. Here is a brief list of just some of the excessive state mandates out there today:

A Sampling of Excessive State Mandates

Acupuncture

Alcoholism treatment

Athletic trainer

Breast reduction

Chiropractor visits

Contraceptives

Dieticians

Drug abuse treatment

Hair prosthesis

Home health care

Hormone replacement therapy

In-vitro fertilization

Marriage therapy

Massage therapy

Morbid obesity treatment

Nature treatments

Pastoral counseling

Port-wine stain elimination

Professional counseling

Smoking cessation

Speech therapy

Varicose vein removal

Needless to say, forcing every insurance company to cover such a broad range of conditions and treatments, whether a customer wants them covered or not, drives up insurers' costs.

That in turn drives up the price of premiums, which has several follow-on effects. Healthy twenty-somethings can't get catastrophe-only policies with low premiums. As premium levels increase, more citizens forego *all* coverage. And costs to companies that provide worker health insurance go up too, putting an insidious downward pressure on wages and employment.[26]

Other state-level regulations also drive up the cost of insurance. Two of the most common rules are "guaranteed issue," which requires insurers to cover anyone and everyone who asks to sign up, and "community rating," which requires companies to set premiums without discriminating on the basis of customers' medical conditions. In effect, there are no limitations for pre-existing conditions. These two rules make it illegal for an insurance provider to turn away a client who is certain to cause the company a financial loss.

Moreover, if you can't be turned down if you climb on the bandwagon only when you are sick, why should you bother wasting money on insurance *until you are sick?*

Imagine if there was a "guaranteed issue" law for fire insurance. Talk about negative selection! No one would buy coverage—unless their homes were actually on fire.

So mandates turn insurance coverage into a great push-me-pull-you beast. States try to force individuals to buy insurance while at the same time providing powerful incentives *not to buy insurance at all.*

Political gold or political poison?

Legislators keep bandying around the idea of universal health insurance as though it were political gold. But once people become aware of the tax increases required to fund it, universal coverage turns out to be not so popular after all. Health insurance mandate laws have failed again and again in state legislatures and with the population.

In 1989, Oregon took the bold step of reforming its health care system with an approach that introduced rationing. Some procedures were made widely available. Others were excluded. Oregonians started out loving the new system. But when people were forced to pay a bit for their coverage, enrollment plunged. Today Oregon's reform effort is rarely mentioned by mandate advocates.[27]

In Illinois, Democratic governor Rod Blagojevich decided to embrace comprehensive health care reform. But the legislature balked at his plan's hefty price tag, voting it down 107 to 0 in 2007.

In Wisconsin, a plan to double the state's taxes to install single-payer health care passed the state Senate but met its demise in the lower legislative chamber.

Even in wealthy Connecticut, politicians also cringed at the price tag of a universal plan.[28]

Republican California governor Arnold Schwarzenegger is yet another leader who says he wants to introduce universal health care. The California Health Care Foundation took a sober look at the Massachusetts example and calculated how much it would cost to replicate in the Golden State where the number of uninsured, at around 6.8 million,[29] is more than the total population of Massachusetts.

The foundation came up with an estimate of nearly $10 billion.[30] So Governor Schwarzenegger backed an implementation plan that proposed "shared responsibility" among employers, providers, insurers, individuals, and government. State legislators thought that was too much sharing, though, and rejected the comprehensive plan. It was not backed by a single Republican legislator.

Instead, they approved only the part of Schwarzenegger's plan that taxed businesses and imposed mandates on insurance companies. Schwarzenegger vetoed the resulting bill, and proposed a new $14-billion bipartisan bill with the Democratic Assembly to bring the Massachusetts plan to California.

Schwarzenegger's plan would have been funded, in part, by a tobacco tax increase. But even if it had passed the legislature, it would still have had to be approved by California voters in November 2008. As of this writing, in October, 2008, Governor Schwarzenegger has not been able to get his universal coverage plan to the residents of California.

A dangerous myth

One fundamental problem with most mandate proposals is that they don't get discussed honestly. When Hillary Clinton was running in the Democratic presidential primary, she frequently touted mandates. Left out of the stump speeches was the cold hard truth of what mandates would actually require.

For those who refused to purchase insurance, the government would garnish wages or withhold tax refunds. For those who couldn't afford to pay, taxpayers would end up footing the bill. That's the real way the newly insured avoid the true cost of the service.

When the beneficiaries of a service are insulated from the cost, and that service is easily available, it's inevitable that expenditures will spiral out of control.[31] To try to keep expenses in check, some form of rationing is required. That usually means limits on access to the priciest medicines and newest technology. Rationing is a standard feature of single-payer systems such as Canada's, as we'll discuss in Myth Ten.

If our learned leaders are going to keep proposing and re-proposing mandated universal health care, the least they can do is be honest about the sacrifices required: Higher taxes, forced premium payments, one-size-fits-all policies, long waiting lists, rationed care, and limited access to cutting-edge medicine. Likely as not, the voters will say "No thanks!"

Myth Seven: Government Prevention Programs Reduce Health Care Costs

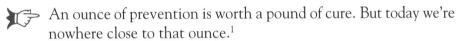 An ounce of prevention is worth a pound of cure. But today we're nowhere close to that ounce.[1]

—Barack Obama

The best treatment is early treatment. The best care is preventative care.[2]

—John McCain

On both sides of the aisle, politicians love to talk about preventative care. Unhealthy behaviors, so the argument goes, raise the cost of health care for everyone. If the government could only do more to discourage or prevent such behaviors, then we'd all pay less.

It's not hard to see why this view is so prevalent. Statistics seem to bear it out.

Recent studies have shown that as much as *75 percent* of what we spend on health care goes to treating conditions brought about by activities such as eating fatty foods and smoking.[3] Nearly

10 percent of the nation's health care dollars are spent annually on diseases attributable to obesity,[4] and an estimated $167 billion go to treat smoking-related illnesses.[5]

Wouldn't we taxpayers save all kinds of money by having the government push programs that dissuade people from smoking too much, drinking too much, and spending hour after hour on their computers or on the couch in front of their TVs?

On the surface, it seems logical to help people stay healthy. But the record shows otherwise. Just like the other myths we've examined so far, state-run programs to "create good health" have had an abysmal payoff. To date, they've not only been hugely unsuccessful, they've often worsened the very problems they set out to solve. And, in the process, they've driven up overall health care costs. They make us less healthy while wasting dollars that could have been better spent.

No child left with a big behind[6]

All around the country, draconian health bans are popping up like PEZ candy. Legislators are tripping over each other to lead the fight against public smoking, soft drink machines in public schools, and trans fats. In July 2008, for instance, the California legislature passed—and Governor Arnold Schwarzenegger signed——a measure banning trans fats in restaurants and other public food facilities.

These new rules don't make it illegal to endanger our own health—after all, this is still a free country—but they deftly sidestep the Constitution by making it ever more expensive and inconvenient to indulge in what the health police find offensive. Such bans can go to ridiculous lengths.

A good example is what might be called a "full disclosure" food bill put forward by Senator Tom Harkin of Iowa in March 2008. The measure would force restaurant chains with more than 20 locations to provide detailed nutritional information on every dish they sell.[7]

So, although you'd still be free to down those delicious cheese fries from an Outback Steakhouse, Senator Harkin's bill would make sure under penalty of law that you were duly warned about how much sin—2,900 calories in this case—you were committing in living your irresponsible life.[8]

The air we breathe

The anti-obesity crusade has been gathering steam for years. It's really a child of the decades-old movement to banish cigarette smoke from just about everywhere. To date, some 3,000 municipalities and most states have enacted restrictions on smoking. Such bans now apply to two-thirds of Americans at some point in their day. The smoking-ban movement has effectively swept the nation.[9]

And smoking bans are rapidly going international. From Canterbury to Kenya, Uruguay to Slovenia, smoking regulations are now part of the air we breathe. These restrictions are rooted in an international consensus that smoking is one of the greatest enemies of good health.[10]

New York mayor Michael Bloomberg and Microsoft founder Bill Gates have pledged $500 million to reduce global smoking rates through education, pushing for more taxes on tobacco products, and even "using religion to help create a social stigma around smoking." As the great reformer Bloomberg warns, "If we do nothing, tobacco will kill one billion people by the end of the century."[11]

Prohibition revisited

The logic behind these kinds of programs follows the great crusades against alcohol in the early twentieth century. It's up to the government to take steps to change people's personal habits—by force if necessary—to make them better citizens and to save society the costs of their addictions. If people would just see the light and act in their own best interests, there would be a reduction in "the wages of sin" and the cost thereof.

In our time when reformers shrink from citing Old Testament hell and damnation, we find the arguments are often made in terms of controlling costs or finding elaborate ways of proving that our behavior is really detrimental to other, innocent people.

By way of fire and brimstone, Senator Hillary Clinton calls the lack of government disease-prevention programs one of the "drivers of health-care costs."[12] From his political pulpit Governor Mike Huckabee thundered that focusing on prevention would save "billions of dollars."[13]

Unfortunately, such overheated rhetoric is not borne out by the facts. People indeed may sicken and die from what they do or do not do. But, as a matter of fact, government-financed attempts to make us healthier rarely do anything to reduce national health care costs.

Even when these programs do—by carrot or stick—get us to eat more healthily or quit smoking, they may actually *increase* long-term costs.

Fat chance

Advocates of government-funded preventative health programs are legion—and loud. Unfortunately, the evidence in support of their much ballyhooed initiatives remains mixed at best.

In 1994, the federal Nutrition Labeling and Education Act man-dated that nutritional and caloric readouts be placed on all pack-aged foods. The idea was that if Americans knew the facts about what they were ingesting, they'd choose to eat healthier.

Yet, since the program was launched and calorie counts began to stare out at us from every bag of Fritos, Americans have become *fatter*. Between 1995 and 2007, the percent of obese Americans increased by two-thirds.[14] Are the reformers on the verge of beginning to ban whole classes of "unhealthy" foods like hotdogs or ice cream?

Smoke signals

What about smoking? Surely informing citizens about the harmful effects of tobacco-smoking will convince more people to quit?

Not quite. According to Dr. Daniel Horn, one of the research-ers who helped coffin-nail the link between smoking and cancer, "You could stand on the rooftop and shout 'smoking is dangerous' at the top of your lungs and you would not be telling anyone any-thing they did not already know."[15]

In fact, not only do smokers know that cigarettes are bad for them, most *overestimate* the health risks. One study found that the average smoker estimates his risk of developing lung cancer to be about 43 percent. In fact, that number is somewhere in the neighborhood of 5 to 10 percent.[16]

So people know smoking is bad for them. And yet they do it any-way because they choose to, not because they are ignorant.

Slapping smokers with taxes isn't the answer either. As a study by Vanderbilt University's W. Kip Viscusi shows, taxes on cigarettes actually create a larger social problem than they solve, since such taxes "impose extremely regressive burdens on the poorest members of society who can least afford to bear the cost."[17]

Despite this, all 50 states plus the District of Columbia impose a levy on cigarettes, ranging from $0.07 per pack in South Carolina to $2.57 in New Jersey.[18] And several states now use cigarette taxes to fund health care programs. In Massachusetts, Governor Deval Patrick signed a measure in July 2008 increasing the state cigarette tax by $1.00 per pack (bringing the levy to $2.51), to help offset the higher-than-expected costs of the former Massachusetts governor Mitt Romney's health insurance law. This, of course, makes the state dependent on smokers. As Massachusetts State Senate Minority Leader Richard Tisei said after the measure was signed, "If you smoke already, please continue to smoke and if you don't smoke, maybe you should start smoking."

As for smoking bans, it's not clear that they do much good, either. Again it's a case of unintended consequences. Thomas Lambert of the University of Missouri argues that stringent smoking bans "may actually increase the incidence of smoking among young people" through what he calls "norm backlash," the common tendency of young people to rebel against the authoritarian forces—read "anti-smoking Puritans"—of their society.[19]

That's right: smoking bans may actually *encourage* young people to smoke.

But this is hardly news. The impotence of anti-smoking campaigns has been established for at least a quarter century. In 1976, the American Cancer Society found that counseling and education programs aimed at reducing the incidence of smoking "had little reported effect on smoking behavior" of adults. As for the young, the organization found that "most attempts . . . have had little success."[20]

But, unlike platform shoes, sideburns, and leisure suits, campaigns against smoking are a '70s fad that, unfortunately, never went out of style.

Shoddy research

Evidence also shows that many government-funded disease-prevention programs are failures. Why is that so?

One reason seems to be that such programs are often based on sloppy, and sometimes dishonest, interpretations of medical research. It seems that when people are convinced they're "doing good for society," they have a strange tendency to be loose with facts.

Take, for instance, Deborah Ortiz, a former California state senator who has been one of the leading advocates for government-run preventative health care legislation. While in office, Ortiz pitched an ambitious ban against sugared soda in California schools. Her bill was based—in part at least—on the aggressive hypothesis that girls who consumed soda were more likely to suffer bone fractures.[21]

The problem? The clinical study on which her legislation was legitimized never benchmarked the bone density of its subjects—and never bothered measuring how much soda the subjects consumed.[22] But science put to work for hyperbole is not humble. Ortiz's bill also boldly claimed that "each additional daily serving of sugar-sweetened soda increases a child's risk for obesity by 60 percent."

A peculiar claim, considering that the author of the study noted that "there is no clear evidence that consumption of sugar per se … causes obesity."[23]

Unfortunately, alarmist assertions by sky-is-falling science-advocates are all too common. John Foreyt, a medical expert from Baylor College, has predicted that, if current trends continue, *every* American will be overweight by 2040.[24]

Even the Terminator is obese

These kinds of patently absurd claims often are creatures of vague or changing definitions. For instance, government standards for what constitutes "overweight" and "obese" are less than scientific.

The standard metric for obesity is called the body-mass index, or BMI. The BMI works by calculating the ratio of an individual's height to weight. Although this sounds straightforward, it often yields inaccurate, implausible, or simply ludicrous results.

According to the government's BMI standards, many professional athletes and Hollywood heartthrobs qualify as overweight. Tom Brady, Brad Pitt, and Matt Damon are all overweight according to the United States government.[25]

It's no wonder the Centers for Disease Control and Prevention can attribute 400,000 deaths per year to obesity, when, in fact, the figure is closer to 26,000 deaths per year:[26] It's a matter of who is doing the measuring and what measures they're using.[27]

However, there's no question that the crisis atmosphere created and perpetuated by bogus research is an effective—and useful— political motivator. That's how vast and overreaching preventative plans like California's ban on trans fats get signed into law. Still, according to the government's standards, the man who signed the law, former bodybuilder Governor Arnold Schwarzenegger, is classified as obese.[28]

Not a financial panacea

It is important to acknowledge that some government-funded prevention programs do in fact promote healthier living.

Such successes, however, rarely if ever translate into decreased health care spending. Quite the contrary, there is mounting evidence that the most successful prevention programs actually make health care *more* expensive.

One obvious reason is that healthier people live longer. Individuals who live into old age require some of the most expensive health care provided to our citizens: late-life care.

As people age, they become more susceptible to illnesses like osteoarthritis, prostate cancer, osteoporosis, and various cognitive illnesses like Alzheimer's disease. These kinds of illnesses make the final years of a person's life incredibly expensive.

A study in the *British Medical Journal* found that in countries with low mortality rates, such as the United States, "elimination of fatal diseases by successful prevention increases health care spending because of the medical expenses during added life years."[29]

We can't play God here, but the cold facts remain that medical spending on a nonsmoker who dies at the average age of 84 is, on average, $100,000 more than spending on a smoker who dies—presumably aided and abetted by his bad habit—at a relatively youthful 77.[30]

Another study published recently in the *New England Journal of Medicine* called the idea that prevention saves health care resources "misleading." While the study conceded that some 19 percent of preventative health measures do save money, it found that "the vast majority reviewed...do not."[31]

These conclusions are indeed cold, but given the wild rhetoric about preventative health care "saving money in the long run," they are not out of line. Time and again research has shown that preventative health care measures in fact raise the overall cost of health care. One study funded by the Dutch Ministry of Health set out to discover whether or not obesity prevention is an effective means of lowering health care costs. The conclusion was blunt and chilling: "Obesity prevention," concluded the researchers, "is not a cure for increasing health expenditures."[32]

The same brutal logic, alas, applies to smoking. In 2001, Philip Morris conducted a study in the Czech Republic to determine whether smokers impose financial burdens on nonsmokers. The answer, not surprisingly, was that they do not. Since smokers don't live as long as non-smokers, they don't burden society with expensive end-of-life care. Thus, smokers save the government money.[33]

Good health is not the yellow brick road to cost savings precisely because of the disproportionate weight of care provided at the far end of life. A recent study in the peer-reviewed journal *PLoS Medicine* showed that, when comparing healthy people, smokers, and the obese, it's the healthy people who end up costing taxpayers the *most*.[34]

Keep such research in mind the next time you hear a politician promising to lower health care costs through government-run preventative medicine programs. Needless to say, quality of life is important, and a value may perhaps be assigned to good living. But if we're genuinely looking to reduce the hard-money costs of health care, prevention is by no means the simple answer.

Soft-serve despotism

In the end, Americans need to decide for themselves: Should we let government take control of our health? If so, to what extent?

The modern preventative health movement started with a few local smoking regulations decades ago. But we are now at the point where regulations govern the number of holes "allowed" in saltshakers.[35] Clearly, things have gone too far. In a sense, we've come full circle. Today's soft-serve despots are yesterday's prohibitionists.

Abraham Lincoln put it best when he spoke out against banning alcohol. "Prohibition will work great injury to the cause of temperance. It is a species of intemperance within itself, for it goes beyond the bounds of reason in that it attempts to control a man's appetite by legislation, and makes a crime out of things that are not crimes. A Prohibition law strikes a blow at the very principles upon which our government was founded."[36]

That was more than 150 years ago, but it's just as relevant today. Lincoln might as well have been talking about banning cheeseburgers or smoking. Government prevention programs don't reduce health care costs. And worse, they are an infringement upon our most basic freedoms.

Myth Eight: We Need More Government to Insure Poor Americans

According to the latest tally from the U.S. Census Bureau, roughly 37 million people in the United States live below the federal poverty level. That's more than 12 percent of the entire U.S. population.[1] Among African-Americans, Latinos, and single mothers, the percentages are even higher.[2]

Making matters worse, poverty rates have not changed much in 40 years, hovering at around 12 percent of the total U.S. population.[3]

Clearly, all these people living in poverty cannot afford to buy health insurance on their own. They need help. And the only way to provide that help on such a massive scale is to expand government health care programs—even if it means squeezing out private sector alternatives.

Or so the argument goes.

Such a line of reasoning may seem logical, but actually it's a huge myth.

In reality, truly poor Americans are already insured by the government. And those who aren't insured simply haven't enrolled in existing government programs.

The last thing these people need is more and larger government health care programs—which, after four decades of trying, have proven to be incapable of providing a level of care that's comparable to what's available through the private sector.

America's poor do *not* go without medical care

Not only can our country's poor not be refused treament, many are already covered by health insurance that's paid for 100 percent by the government.

Any poor person can walk into any hospital in America and be treated for an accident, injury, or disease. According to the federal Emergency Medical Treatment and Active Labor Act, passed in 1986, hospitals are not allowed to deny treatment to patients with no health insurance. The costs of such care—given free to poor patients who have neither insurance nor resources to pay—are routinely absorbed into a hospital's operating costs.

Moreover, many of the country's 37 million poor are already eligible for medical treament paid for completely by the government. Those who aren't covered simply haven't enrolled in existing government programs. The poor, as we saw in Myth Three, it should be noted, are not necessarily the same as those who choose to go without health insurance.

The vast majority of the very poor and disabled are already eligible for state-administered Medicaid programs subsidized—between one-half and two-thirds, depending on the state—by the federal government. Meanwhile, uninsured children from low-income families that earn too much to qualify for Medicaid are eligible for coverage under the State Children's Health Insurance Plan or SCHIP.

So the poor in America today are already covered—or eligible to be covered—under Medicaid. Originally set up as a safety net in 1965, Medicaid has grown into an enormous welfare program, serving 53 million Americans.[4] In other words, Medicaid already covers some 15 million more people than the 37 million estimated to be living in poverty, and almost 10 million more than Medicare.[5] In 2006, individual states and the federal government paid out an estimated $338 billion on such coverage.[6]

It would seem logical, then, to take a long hard look at how the poor are doing under existing Medicaid programs.

Substandard care

It has been almost half a century since Medicaid was created. Yet the care that's delivered through this government program clearly falls short of the standards most Americans are used to receiving through private insurance plans.

At the simplest level, let's compare outcomes.

If you're poor and covered by Medicaid and you have a heart attack, what does the evidence show? Your chances of recovery are lower than if you were covered either by private insurance or by Medicare.

Of course, the poor patients covered by Medicaid tend to be sicker. They have usually received less preventative care over the course of their lives. That may, of course, be at their own choosing.

But the simple fact is, heart-attack patients for whom Medicaid is the primary carrier are significantly less likely to receive immediate care. And they are more likely to die.[7]

Shunned by doctors

Medicaid patients also have a much harder time finding primary care doctors.

Doctors are just opting out of programs like Medicaid since reimbusement rates don't cover costs and there are so many more hassles getting paid.[8] Medicaid programs are administered separately state-by-state, and they're only partially funded by the federal government. Because states have limited budgets, they often try to control costs by putting restrictions on their reimbursement levels to doctors.

In some states, the reimbursement levels are absurdly low. In New York, for example, a doctor earns just $20 for an hour-long consultation with an established Medicaid patient.

As a result, doctors are extremely reluctant to accept Medicaid patients. In a 2003 study by the Medicare Payment Advisory Commission, only 69.5 percent of the primary care physicians and specialists surveyed said they would accept new Medicaid patients.[9] That's a rate six times higher than for Medicare patients and five times higher than for patients with private insurance.[10]

Driving up costs

Medicaid's low reimbursement rates may save the government a few bucks in the short-term. But over the long run, they actually drive up the overall cost of care—raising prices for everyone and ultimately making medical services even less accessible to the poor.

"Note to Medicaid Patients: The Doctor Won't See You"

"Jada Garrett, a 16-year-old sophomore, developed what seemed at first a mild case of strep throat. Within a couple of weeks her joints ballooned. Many afternoons, her swollen ankles hurt too much to walk. To get to the bottom of her symptoms, Jada needed to see a rheumatologist. But the local one listed in her Medicaid plan's network wouldn't see her in his office. The wait to get into a clinic was more than three months. By the time she found a rheumatologist in a nearby county to take her in mid-April, Jada's debilitating pain caused her to miss several weeks of school. 'You feel so helpless thinking, something's wrong with this child and I can't even get her into a doctor,' says Jada's mother, Nicole Garrett, who enrolled her three teenage daughters in Medicaid after they lost private coverage. 'When we had real insurance, we could call and come in at the drop of a hat.'…. when Medicaid patients seek care, they often find themselves locked out of the medical system…. That's because many Medicaid programs, straining under surging costs, are balancing their budgets by freezing or reducing payments to doctors. That in turn is driving many doctors, particularly specialists, out of the program."

–Vanessa Fuhrmans, *Wall Street Journal*.[11]

Walk into any urban hospital emergency department (ED), and you'll see Medicaid patients using ED services for non-emergency problems. They may be forced to wait for hours, but EDs cannot legally refuse to provide care—even though care provided in an emergency room is far more expensive than care in a doctor's office or community or retail clinic.

In trying to save money, the government has created a vicious circle. Because it's often too difficult for Medicaid patients to find a doctor, they end up going to expensive emergency rooms, where they can't be turned away.

When Medicaid patients do find non-ED care, it's often through "Medicaid mills," where patients are treated in volume on a fee-for-service basis that maximizes throughput. Such facilities tend to provide marginal care. Waiting rooms are crowded, waits are long, the staff is impersonal, and the time actually spent with a physician may be just minutes.

Not surprisingly, Americans overwhelmingly prefer private health care over government coverage. A Commonwealth survey found that 65 percent of citizens, whether or not they were currently insured, would rather have private coverage. Only 10 percent would want Medicaid or Medicare.[12]

The poor may have coverage, but the quality of care that's actually provided is far from ideal.

An interesting program was established in 2007 at the University of Chicago Medical Center that directs patients who don't have private medical insurance—primarily the poor and African-Americans—to other facilities. Michelle Obama, who was on unpaid leave during the presidential campaign, was involved in the creation of the program.

The program is called the Urban Health Initiative. Its goal is to locate neighborhood doctors for low-income individuals who are causing overcrowding at the University of Chicago Medical Center's emergency room for basic treatment. Hospital officials said that these patients make it difficult for them to focus on the critically ill who are in need of specialized care such as cancer treatment and organ transplants.

The idea is that the initative together with a companion program called the South Side Collaborative will dramatically improve care for thousands of South Side residents. Rather than waiting hours at the U of C's emergency room, the patients will be seen faster and at less expense at neighborhood clinics and other hospitals.[13]

Bankrupting the country

Not only is the quality of health care received under Medicaid subpar, but the program itself is outrageously expensive.

In fact, the costs of Medicaid are already out of control and on the verge of bankrupting state governments around the country. And the program is also placing an enormous strain on the federal government, which on average picks up 57 percent of Medicaid's tab, although that figure varies by state.[14]

Outlays for Medicaid amount to 22 percent of state spending and have surpassed even education as the number one drain on state budgets.[15] And that's just the national average.

In Medicaid-heavy states like Florida, the program is projected to consume nearly 60 percent of the state's budget by 2015.

In South Carolina, roughly 20 percent of the state's population is already on Medicaid, including 30 percent of seniors and 40 percent of children. One out of every two births is paid for by Medicaid, which is expected to gobble up 24 percent of the state's budget by 2010.[16]

All across the nation, the very old, even those who are middle class are also turning to Medicaid for nursing homes as they outlive other coverages.[17]

These costs are not financially sustainable. Yet perversely, because up to three federal dollars come to a state for every dollar it pays out in Medicaid, most states are actively seeking to expand Medicaid-type spending as a source of funds.[18]

Rampant fraud

Since states receive open-ended matching funds from the federal government on their Medicaid outlays, they have incentives to game the federal government. Many misuse Medicaid monies by dropping it into their pool of general revenue.[19]

☞ A single bureaucrat in Buffalo enrolled 4,434 students in Medicaid-sponsored speech therapy in one day, giving state taxpayers a massive bill. This practice is common in school districts and, according to a federal audit, cost taxpayers $1.2 billion from 1993 to 2001.[20]

☞ Dr. Mikhail Makhlin routinely prescribed $6,400 a month of AIDS drugs to perfectly healthy people who, in turn, sold the drugs on the black market. This scheme cost taxpayers $11.5 million from 2000 to 2003.[21]

☞ Private insurance doesn't pay for cab rides to the doctor's office, but Medicaid does. The catch: patients are supposed to be unable to walk. This is clearly violated hundreds of times daily as people walk to taxpayer-funded ambulettes charging as much as $31 one way for transportation to the doctor's office. A Brooklyn massage therapist makes use of 90 trips a day for patients. A single patient used 153 trips in one year. "It's old people," one expert told the New York Times, "They want to come every day because they are bored at home."[22]

With its myriad rules and lax enforcement, most experts also agree that Medicaid is riddled by fraud and misspending. Unfortunately, no one even knows how much money is lost every year by misuse of Medicaid funds, but fraud is frequently estimated to consume at least 10 percent of outlays.[23]

And the problem is only getting worse. So long as states keep cramming more people under the government health care umbrella, costs will continue to rocket skyward.

Arbitrary and unresponsive

Today's Medicaid has grown helter-skelter to fit wildly diverse groups—infants, children, parents, pregnant women, the disabled, seniors, and even many middle-class Americans who need long-term care.

As a result, it's a patchwork filled with perverse incentives, gaping holes in coverage for enrollees, and structural inefficiencies.

Coverage varies state by state, often without rhyme or reason. Under original Medicaid rules, for instance, drug coverage by individual states was an optional benefit.[24] Yet who could say that drug coverage is optional today for some patients? In fact, denial of such coverage may massively *increase* ultimate costs.

Often, the arbitrary rules about what's covered and what isn't can be a matter of life and death.

Consider the plight of Memphis native Phyllis Denise Coleman, who was profiled in the Memphis *Commercial Appeal* in July 2008.[25] Divorced and 49 years of age, she suffers from sarcoidosis, an inflammatory disease that attacks the lungs. To survive, she uses an oxygen machine 24 hours a day, which has been paid for by TennCare, the Medicaid managed care program of Tennessee.

Abruptly in April 2008, Denise received a summary notice from TennCare to the effect that her coverage was being terminated because of administrative changes.

"Coleman's terminal illness and her dependence on oxygen don't make a difference, said TennCare spokeswoman Marilyn Wilson," according to the *Commercial Appeal*.

Clearly, Medicaid is hardly a paragon of good customer service.

Paperwork costs

It's often argued that Medicaid administrative costs are lower than those of the private sector. No discussion of Medicaid would be complete without debunking this mini-myth.

According to the American Academy of Family Physicians (AAFP), for example, "Medicaid Administrative Costs (MACs) are among the lowest of any health care payer in the country."[26] The AAFP puts Medicaid's administrative costs at 4 to 6 percent, compared to around 15 to 20 percent for a well-run private insurance company. Similar claims from journalists and politicians are ubiquitous.

But these statements are deeply misleading. For starters, they completely ignore the fact that Medicaid dumps many of its administrative costs on the private sector. The IRS does the same thing—forcing the taxpayers to do all the expensive paperwork.

Doctors and other health care providers spend countless hours— and therefore dollars— filling out government forms and complying with thousands of pages of regulations. Those costs may not show up in Medicaid's books, but providers feel them acutely, and they drive prices up.

Unfortunately, the administrative costs that doctors and hospitals incur to get paid are simply not put into the calculation. Nor do

Medicaid estimates take into consideration the huge costs imposed upon patients in the form of lower-quality, rationed health care.

Several years ago, the Council for Affordable Health Insurance published a study, which found that when all of the hidden costs and certain related unfunded liabilities were included, Medicare and Medicaid administrative costs were significantly higher (26.9 percent) than the private sector (16.2 percent).[27]

Underming the future

One of the biggest problems with Medicaid is that—like all government safety nets—it encourages risky behavior. That risky behavior, in turn, results in more people falling into the safety net. And the program becomes an ever increasing burden.

That's exactly what's happening today.

Think about it this way. If you know the government will come to the rescue even if you can't afford health care, then why save for the future? In fact, why would anyone set aside resources for retirement when he can get "free" coverage? This "moral hazard" has resulted in a vortex that's steadily sucking more and more people into Medicaid.

Medicaid for millionaires

One of the fastest growing and most expensive parts of Medicaid is long-term nursing home and end-of-life care for the elderly. Nearly 80 percent of residents in nursing facilities now rely on Medicaid or Medicare subsidies.[28]

With crafty estate planning and schemes to protect assets, increasing numbers of the middle-class elderly are intentionally becoming "poor" to qualify for long-term care at taxpayer expense. Instead of planning to cover their own long-term care with private insurance, they are switching to free Medicaid, undercutting the demand for private long-term care insurance.[29]

In fact, there are lawyers who actually specialize in helping wealthy clients hide their assets in order to qualify for Medicaid. Through this "Medicaid for millionaires" scheme, even the very wealthy are foisting their nursing home bills onto taxpayers.[30]

Medicaid is well on its way to becoming a welfare program for middle-income families. And, of course, this leaves fewer resources for the truly poor, whom the program was originally intended to serve.

No model of excellence

The claim that we need more government to provide health care to the poor is a false one. The fact is, the government already does provide coverage to the poor. It has been doing so for more than 40 years. And the results are hardly encouraging.

Our nation's experience with Medicaid is not a happy one. The quality of care that patients receive under the program is exceedingly poor. The vast majority of Americans would prefer private coverage. And ballooning Medicaid costs are now threatening to bankrupt states across the nation.

Meanwhile, the problem is getting worse. Medicaid has grown beyond just the poor. Middle-class Americans are incorporating this program into their retirement planning—and certain politicians are now pushing to expand it to the middle-class Americans.

None of this is to say that Medicaid doesn't provide an important safety net. It does, especially for the truly poor and disabled. But the system is hardly a model of excellence, and the last thing this country needs is to expand it.

Myth Nine: Health Information Technology Is a Silver Bullet for Reducing Costs

 By computerizing health records, we can avoid dangerous medical mistakes, reduce costs, and improve care.[1]

—President George W. Bush

When it comes to reforming health care, we can all agree on two things: First, more Americans need better access to medical care. Second, one of the easiest ways to improve access is to make that care more affordable.

If only we could agree on how to achieve those goals.

There seem to be as many political solutions to the rising costs of health care as there are "miraculous" weight loss products. So when both sides of the aisle in Congress agree on a way to drive down health care costs, it would seem to be a reason to celebrate.

You might want to read on before you break out the Dom Pérignon.

Health Information Technology (HIT) is frequently touted by members of both partes as a silver bullet for reducing rising medical costs. A typical remark comes from, one of the country's most prominent HIT proponents. In a September 2006 interview, for instance, former Speaker of the House Newt Gingrich claimed that "[h]ealth IT has been proven to have enormous potential to transform our health system into one marked by efficiency, quality, and safety."[2]

Is this initiative, little known to the average citizen, about to bring our skyrocketing bills back down to earth?

Not quite. Unfortunately, you can't legislate technological innovation.

What's all the fuss about?

So what exactly is this so-called silver bullet?

On the simplest level, HIT is a concept—the idea that by using technology, we can drive down health costs.

This notion certainly holds true for other industries. Think of personal computers. Prices have plummeted over the past 30 years, even as processing speeds have increased at geometric rates.

Or look at the telephone industry. In 1984, a long-distance phone call cost 28 cents per minute—and mobile phones were the stuff of James Bond movies. Today, I can make a long-distance call for a few pennies on my cell phone—which, incidentally, has more processing power than the 8-bit desktop computer back in 1984.[3]

There's no denying that the health care business is lagging in its adoption of the information technologies that have made so many other industries dramatically more efficient.

Next time you walk into a doctor's office or a hospital, see if the filing system is computerized. There's a good chance you'll see a wall lined with thousands of manila folders. That's common practice in the medical world. In fact, 90 percent of U.S. doctors and more than two-thirds of hospitals still keep their patient records on good-old-fashioned paper.[4]

Imagine how much money could be saved —and efficiencies created—by accelerating the introduction of technology into the medical world. Translating those benefits over to the health care industry seems like a no-brainer.

Not surprisingly, politicians think to themselves: Why bicker endlessly over modest funding increases and difficult cuts in entitlement programs when we can let computers solve the problem?

And that's exactly what they've decided to do.

An ambitious plan

In 2004, President George W. Bush outlined an ambitious plan "to ensure that most Americans have electronic health records within the next 10 years."[5]

He envisioned a brave new world in which patients could visit any physician's office and all their personal information, allergies, medications, and medical history would be instantly available.

Parents wouldn't have to carry around boxes of their children's medical records and old X-rays. They could simply authorize a new doctor to retrieve that information electronically from a previous physician.

Everything would be digital. If you showed up at an emergency room, doctors could pull up your information on a computer and immediately access your medical history to learn what pills you take, so as to avoid any dangerous drug interactions.

With all this information processed and shared electronically, the government could even monitor for disease outbreaks or bio-terror attacks.[6]

The Bush administration wants the United States to have a national electronic health care infrastructure by 2014. To help our country develop that infrastructure, the president has even established a National Health Information Technology Coordinator at the Department of Health and Human Services.[7]

But can the government pull it off?

Few would argue that by adopting better technology, the health care industry could improve productivity, reduce errors, and save costs.

But here's the problem: That exact same argument can be made for virtually any industry or business.

By adopting better technology, a bubble-gum factory could also improve productivity, reduce errors, and save costs. So could a local police station. Or a restaurant. Or a law firm.

Businesses—including those in the health care industry—are constantly struggling to adopt more advanced technologies so they can better compete in the open marketplace.

So the real question we should be asking is not whether a techno-logical revolution in health care would be beneficial, but whether government is capable of creating such a revolution. And whether it's even government's role to try.

An even bigger concern is that by trying to create a technology "solution," the government could, in fact, slow down technological innovation and progress in the health care industry.

Our government does not have a successful track record in this area. In 1996, Congress passed the Health Insurance Portability and Accountability Act (HIPAA). Back then, politicians raved about how this law would bring about a new age in medicine, where individuals had portable electronic health records.

Well, guess what? In more than 10 years, it still hasn't happened. We don't have portable, secure electronic health records. But the law sure created a nice boondoggle for lawyers and consultants.[8]

This isn't *Star Trek*

The sad reality is that as much as we'd like for politicians to be able to create technological revolutions, they just aren't very good at it. The high-tech transformations we've witnessed in various industries have been brought about by private companies.

A government program didn't invent the miracle cancer-fighting drug Rituxan for fighting non-Hodgkin's lymphoma. A private company did.[9] Similarly, private firms like Microsoft and Google are also driving technological innovation. Incidentally, both companies are already in the process of rolling out their own products to facilitate electronic health records.

It would be amazing if your doctor could review your CAT scan on his iPhone. But that doesn't mean the government should create a program to subsidize and encourage doctors to buy iPhones. We can't legislate our way into a *Star Trek* world of health care.

Just look at any other industry where the government calls the shots from on-high. Take your local Department of Motor Vehicles (DMV). Invariably, the technology lags far behind what they have in the local Toyota dealership. And the same can be said of the U.S. Postal Service compared to a private company like UPS, DHL, or FedEx.

Private businesses are quite good at adopting the right technology at the right time—and finding innovative solutions to improve productivity. When government tries to grease that process, it often gums up the gears. You end up with something resembling a classroom in a D.C. public high school. There are plenty of computers, but not enough textbooks, or even kids who can read.

There are sound reasons to be skeptical about a government-engineered HIT revolution. All too often very real problems are glossed over in the health care debate, in favor of pie-in-the-sky utopian visions about the potential of technology to lower costs and save lives.

What savings?

Politicians love to talk about HIT as though it will automatically save costs—like some kind of electronic slot machine that's guaranteed to hit the jackpot. If hospitals and doctors just buy a ton of fancy computers, they'll save money hand over fist.

In reality, it's not so simple. A 2005 study by the RAND Corporation concluded that HIT could save our health care system around $77 billion a year, assuming it's properly implemented and widely adopted.[10] Barack Obama often cites this study.

Now that seems like a lot of money in savings, but it's not so much if you think of it relative to our total health care investment.

Americans spend *$2.3 trillion* a year on health care. So potential savings as a result of HIT are only 3.3 percent of our total medical spending.

That's like a family cutting its housing costs by moving from a house with 21 rooms to a house with 20.

What are the costs for hospitals?

Still, a savings of 3.3 percent annually is nothing to sneeze at, and few dispute that implementing HIT systems and switching to electronic medical records will save money in the long run.

But the decision to outfit a physician's practice or a hospital with new technology is not a simple one.

The upfront cost of implementing a good HIT system is absolutely enormous—especially for hospitals.

The Washington Hospital Center in Washington, D.C., has been using an HIT system called Azyxxi for over 10 years. The sticker price for this system: $150 million.

Across town, the George Washington University (GW) hospital has implemented its HIT system for somewhere under $300 million, according to one administrator. As a result, it's saving about $1 million a year.[11]

It's tough to make those numbers fly. If GW spent nearly $300 million and is saving only $1 million a year, then its HIT system is hardly the world's greatest investment.

With many hospitals already overextended and losing money, such large expenditures need to be weighed and measured carefully.

In particular, those expenditures need to be balanced against other potential investments.

Could $150 million be better spent on improving patient care more directly by upgrading outdated medical equipment, hiring more doctors and general practitioners, alleviating emergency room waiting lines, or opening up more beds in crowded wards?

Doctors and hospital administrators are far better equipped to know the answer to that question than bureaucrats in Washington.

Moreover, when politicians distort the economic realities underlying those decisions—by creating regulations that encourage HIT investments over other expenditures—a hospital might end up buying a computer when what it really needs is a dialysis machine.

What about smaller practices?

Making the transition from paper to computerized records isn't cheap for individual doctors, either. It costs anywhere from $40,000 to $60,000 for an individual doctor or small practice to make the switch.[12] Plus, many older doctors are not computer savvy like young graduates who grew up with computers.

As a result, many doctors—like hospitals—are biding their time.

The government is trying to speed things up by throwing cash at these doctors.

In 2008, the Department of Health and Human Services (HHS) started a $150-million program to pay doctors in certain areas up to $58,000 to computerize their records. It will pay larger practices up to $290,000.

HHS is now trying to get Congress to expand the program by another $50 million.[13]

The Department of Veterans Affairs spends roughly $450 million annually maintaining an electronic records database for its medical system. Programmers have developed an open-source version of the VA software, and have made it available to private hospitals and private physician practices.[14]

These are great deals for doctors, but should taxpayers be forced to subsidize this so-called technology revolution? Shouldn't physicians have to buy their own software just like professionals in other industries? It's not as if they don't earn enough money to purchase computers. And computers are a business expense.

No rush to implement

Given the high cost, it's not surprising that doctors and hospitals aren't exactly rushing to implement HIT systems. In fact, only five percent of hospitals and 10 percent of doctors had completely made the switch by late 2006.[15]

But with government promoting HIT so aggressively, then surely state-run hospitals are leading the charge, right?

Wrong.

Despite the active role the government has taken in promoting HIT, state-run hospitals are lagging behind private hospitals considerably when it comes to adopting it.

A February 2007 report by the software security company Citrix Systems found that just 19 percent of state health care systems had begun using electronic medical records, compared with 54 percent of private hospitals.[16]

If government is lagging behind, do we really want it to lead the way?

A mountain of red tape

Switching from manila folders to an electronic record-keeping system is one thing. But networking thousands of hospitals, doctors' offices, and laboratories will be a monumental task. Putting the government in charge of such a massive and complex endeavor is to guarantee a regulatory mess.[17]

There are currently at least 12 different federal agencies with overlapping oversight when it comes to health care technology.[18] This dirty dozen already produces mountains of red tape and conflicting rules that govern the use of HIT.

This is hardly the best way to spur HIT innovation. With all these different governing bodies, private IT companies have an even harder time creating solutions—because their products need to comply with a morass of regulations. Instead, they should be free to create products that doctors and patients actually want, as opposed to what the government wants.

Could bureaucrats have dreamed of Microsoft?

For his part, current HHS Secretary Mike Leavitt has attempted to jumpstart lackluster HIT innovation in private industry with partnerships between HHS and private companies.

In 2005, HHS announced $18.6 million in contracts to four well-known private firms—Accenture, the Computer Sciences Corporation, I.B.M., and Northrop Grumman. The goal was to build HIT infrastructure in 12 regions of the U.S. that HHS hoped would serve as "models for the nation," according to the *New York Times*.[19]

Three years later, Leavitt announced that Medicare would make $150 million over five years available directly to doctors and health care agencies to adopt HIT in another selected 12 communities.[20]

It might seem like an ideal partnership between government initiative and private know-how. HHS's former HIT coordinator Dr. David J. Brailer insists, "This is a hands-off government approach. We're not operating these networks, and we're not procuring them."

Yet, it's hard not to be skeptical of the government's involvement here. It's one thing for an HIT product to succeed as a result of competition in the marketplace; it's quite another for an HIT product to be the outcome of complying with complex government-mandated specifications.

Driving innovation from the top down by tempting potential innovators with cash is one way to jumpstart an industry. But it's rarely as effective in producing the needed quality and range of products —in this case, information technology products—as letting businesses respond to demands from the real market.

Picture how the computer industry might have evolved if the government had been in charge of it.

We would have a computer in every government office, but would we be likely to have a computer in every home? Why would bureaucrats have ever dreamed of the usefulness of such a thing? Even other computer geeks laughed at Microsoft's Bill Gates when he predicted it would happen.

Letting innovators innovate

Fortunately, we don't need government to bribe companies to innovate. The $2.3 trillion health care marketplace is already an enormous opportunity for the information technology sector— and private companies realize this.

Even now, the IT industry's leaders are moving into health care products. In February of 2008, Google announced that a service was forthcoming that would allow people to track and monitor their health records.[21] In June 2008, Kaiser Permanente and Microsoft announced that they were collaborating on a consumer-driven approach to medical records.[22]

These companies have seen an unfulfilled market and they're working to try to serve it.

Companies like Microsoft and Google, with proven track records as IT innovators—giving people what they didn't even know they wanted—are far more likely to tap the full potential of HIT than government contractors.

However impatient politicians are to see increased HIT usage, they should stay out of the marketplace and let these companies do what they do best—find needs and satisfy them.

Somewhere down the road, advancements in HIT may truly revolutionize medicine and make it more affordable. It's already starting to happen. The irony is that by trying to speed up HIT innovation, government may end up slowing it down—and costing taxpayers a boatload of money in the process.

Myth Ten: Government-Run Health Care Systems in Other Countries are Better and Cheaper than America's

It's a fact that the United States spends more on health care—both as a percentage of its gross domestic product and on a per-capita basis—than any other nation in the world.[1] Yet when it comes to certain high-profile health care indicators, America seems to lag far behind. As *New York Times* columnist Paul Krugman once put it, "America's health care system spends more, for worse results, than that of any other advanced country."[2]

Through Krugman's pessimistic bifocals, his claim may seem quite convincing.

Take infant mortality. Defined as the number of infant deaths per 1,000 live births, a nation's infant mortality rate has long been considered a basic yardstick of its health care system and overall health levels. According to the *2008 CIA World Factbook*, the United States ranks 42nd in the world, behind such unlikely competitors as Portugal, Slovenia, Malta, the Czech Republic, and even Cuba.[3]

Or consider life expectancy, another oft-cited measure. Here, the United States comes in a dismal 29th—behind medical power-houses like Bosnia and Herzegovina, Jordan, and Cyprus.[4]

On top of these hardly stellar rankings, critics love to point out that the United States is the only wealthy, industrialized nation in the world that doesn't provide universal health care for all its citizens.[5] This is seen by a moral failing by some.

These sickly stats explain why, in its listing of international health care systems, the World Health Organization (WHO) puts the United States at an unflattering 37th out of 191 countries. According to WHO's diligent researchers, Costa Rica, Morocco, and Cyprus have better health care systems than the United States.

And of course there is no shortage of enlightened analysts who seize upon such "facts" to claim that socialized medicine is much better at taking care of all the people's medical needs. Only by seeing the light and adopting government health insurance, these critics argue, do Americans have even a glimmer of a chance of improving patient outcomes and cutting costs.

It just isn't so. As Josh Billings, an American humorist, once quipped, "it ain't ignorance that causes the trouble in the world. It's the things people know that ain't so." The ideologues who use these arguments are massively and obviously *wrong*. Only by keeping a set of full-metal blinders in place can they come up with these *Alice in Wonderland* conclusions based on what we might call Mad Hatter manipulations of data.

Because the truth is exactly the reverse. It is government monop-oly health care that is heartless and uncaring. And the inferior treatments it provides come with a very steep price tag—rationed care, lack of access to tests, with the latest technological equipment, and long waiting lists.

A personal story

In 2003, my uncle, a Canadian who lived in Vancouver, was diagnosed with non-Hodgkin's lymphoma, a cancer of the lymphatic system. Living in the United States at the time, I began investigating possible treatments, hoping that something other than standard chemotherapy might help.

I soon discovered that a new drug called Rituxan had shown great promise in fighting NHL in the United States. But it wasn't yet available in Canada, so my uncle couldn't get it.

The doctor suggested that if my uncle wanted to try Rituxan, he should start commuting to Seattle, Washington, a two-and-a-half-hour drive south of Vancouver. But he was elderly and decided he didn't have the energy to make such trips. Six months later he was dead. Had he lived in America, he might have survived.

That wasn't the only time I had a troubling confrontation with Canada's health care system. Medical authorities in Canada decided that my ailing mother was too old and too sick to merit the highest quality care. She, along with other weak and elderly Canadians, were hastened to their fates by actuarial calculations in what is truly a dehumanizing system of triage.

Neither of these incidents is isolated. When the government pays for health care, saving money can easily become a more pressing concern than saving lives.

A lesson in economics

"Unlike other advanced countries," pontificates Paul Krugman, "we treat access to health care as a privilege rather than a right."

A "right" to health care sure sounds nice, but there's no medical Tooth Fairy. Goods and services are not free. Doctors, nurses, and hospital staffers cost money. So do drugs, MRI machines, and latex gloves.

If health care were free and available with no regard to cost, people could go to the doctor as often as they pleased. But, unfortunately, economies—not to mention taxpayers—might well sink under the weight of such unlimited demand.

No responsibility whatsoever. Think about that. Instead of watching what you eat, you'd just go for "free" gastric bypass surgery. Instead of watching your alcohol consumption, you'd take advantage of a "free" liver transplant. Instead of not smoking, just replace your lungs on your 45th birthday. And if you need or want drugs, then the sky's the limit. Stock up on Lipitor, Xanax, and Ritalin.

Free restaurants would be nice, too. Why would anyone go to the trouble of dragging home groceries and wasting time cooking? Why would anyone not go for the best? The only thing is, someone would have to pay. Consumption would rise, and so would costs.

It's the basics of economics. Maybe sunshine is free. But just about everything else costs. There has to be some mechanism for matching limited supply with potentially unlimited demand.

So even if health care is declared a "right" by Mr. Krugman and others, someone pays. And when a service isn't allocated by prices in a free market, then it has to be rationed.

That's exactly what happens under government medicine, and people subjected to such rationing quickly become familiar with this economic reality.

Access to a waiting list is not access to health care

It's not just drug rationing that hastens the deaths of the ill and the elderly. Socialized systems ration services across the whole range of medical care. In Canada that means limited access to physicians, surgery, and other procedures needed by ordinary Canadians every day.

In Canada today, where slightly more than 33 million people live,[6] more than 800,000 citizens are currently on waiting lists for surgery and other necessary treatments. Fifteen years ago the average wait between a referral from a primary care doctor and treatment by a specialist was around nine weeks. Today that wait is more than 18 weeks.[7]

That's almost double what doctors consider clinically reasonable. As Brian Day, a Canadian physician and immediate past president of the Canadian Medical Association, explained to the *New York Times*, Canada "is a country in which dogs can get a hip replacement in under a week and in which humans can wait two to three years."[8]

In part, these waits are due to a doctor shortage. According to the Organization for Economic Cooperation and Development (OECD), Canada ranks 24th out of 28 countries in doctors per thousand people. When the government took over the health care system in the early 1970s, Canada ranked second.[9]

Indeed, many Canadians can't even find a doctor. About 10 percent are currently seeking a primary care physician. "It's like winning the lottery to get in and see the doctor," explained Marcel Brunelle, the mayor of Whitby, Ontario.

In some provinces, there actually *is* a lottery. In Nova Scotia, health officials have resorted to using a lottery to determine who gets to see a doctor.

A Five-Year Wait in Sault St. Marie

A 31-year old man and his wife moved to Sault St. Marie, Canada, to be closer to her family. When he tried to make an appointment for a physical, he was told that he would have to wait for five years. But the administrator told him that if he "knew someone" who could pull some strings, his waiting time might be less. He never did get that physical in Sault St. Marie but instead drove to Detroit and paid for his physical out of pocket.

What's up, doc?

Why so few doctors? Over the past decade, about 11 percent of physicians trained in Canadian medical schools have moved to the United States. That's because doctors' salaries in Canada are negotiated, set, and paid for by provincial governments and held down by cost-conscious budget analysts. Today, in fact, the average Canadian doctor earns only 42 percent of what a doctor earns in the United States. Because the cost of training doctors at medical schools in Canada is very expensive, the government finds it cheaper to bring in International Medical Graduates (IMGs) from countries like Pakistan and India than to train Canadians to be doctors.

Canada also limits access to common medical technology. When compared to other OECD countries, Canada is 13th out of 24 in access to MRIs, 18th of 24 in access to CT scanners, and seventh of 17 in access to mammograms.[10] That lack of access is why Canada has seen a 9-percent decline in breast cancer screening for middle-aged women.[11]

And even though it provides "free" health care, the Canadian government doesn't provide universal prescription drug coverage. The Canada Health Act, the federal law that guarantees health coverage, only requires each province to cover drugs delivered to patients in the hospital. Provincial prescription drug coverage plans differ, but about two in three Canadians pay out-of-pocket for drugs. Private insurance is also available for services not covered under the Canada Health Act.

The problems plaguing Canada's health care system—long lines, lack of access to the latest technological equipment, and dwindling doctor supply—are unavoidable in a single-payer system.

These are the hidden costs of government-provided health care, also known as socialized medicine, and these costs are why George Zeliotis, a retired salesman from Montreal, took the Quebec government to court a few years ago.

Faced with the prospect of waiting an entire year for a hip replacement, Zeliotis attempted to make arrangements with his doctor, Jacques Chaoulli, to pay privately for surgery. But that would have been illegal. So he went to court, arguing that while his wait saved the government money, it cost him plenty in pain and endangered his life. Zeliotis lost in two Quebec provincial courts, but the Canadian Supreme Court agreed to hear his appeal—and in June 2005, the court ruled in his favor.[12]

The decision overturned the ban on private health insurance in Quebec, opening the door to private sector participation—and legal challenges—across Canada. Writing for the court, Madame Chief Justice Beverly McLachlin stated, "Access to a waiting list is not access to health care."[13] Madame Justice Marie Deschamps later added that a public health monopoly without waiting lists is virtually an oxymoron.[14]

Stronach Travels to U.S. for Cancer Treatment

"Belinda Stronach, former liberal member of parliament and cabinet minister, traveled outside Canada's health-care system to California for some of her breast cancer treatment.... Stronach...went to California... at her Toronto doctor's suggestion.... Speed was not the issue, [her spokesman Greg] MacEachern said—it was more to do with the type of surgery she and her doctor agreed was best for her, and where it was best performed.... It is unusual for a federal politician to travel outside Canada for private medical treatment, especially given the hallowed status of the Canadian, publicly financed health-care system in the realm of political debate."

—Susan Delacourt, *The Star* (Toronto).[15]

The story is the same in Europe

Canada's problems are not unique—they're characteristic of all government health care systems.

In November 2006, the world learned of Dennis Burke, a 68-year-old Briton suffering from colon cancer. Although the cancer was in remission, he still required check-ups. His general practitioner referred him to a hospital for a consultation. More than a year later, however, Burke still hadn't gotten into the hospital. His "free" check-up had been cancelled 48 times in a row.[16]

Dennis Burke isn't alone. More than one million Britons in need of medical care are currently waiting for hospital admission.[17] Another 200,000 are waiting to get on a waiting list.[18] Each year, Britain's National Health Service (NHS) cancels around 100,000 operations.[19]

Further, Britain's hospitals are in complete disrepair. Every year, more than 100,000 patients contract illnesses and infections that they didn't have prior to admission to NHS hospitals.[20] According to Britain's Malnutrition Advisory Group, up to 40 percent of NHS patients are undernourished while in the hospital.[21]

In France, the story is the same. Just look at the results of the heat wave in August 2003. It took the lives of 15,000 elderly citizens. Because of a shortage of doctors, hospitals were stretched beyond their limit.[22]

Sweden's waiting lists have led some patients to visit veterinarians.[23] As perverse as that sounds, it makes perfect sense—Swedish patients in need of heart surgery are often forced to wait as long as 25 weeks.[24]

Cutting costs cuts lives

Britain even has a government agency explicitly tasked with limiting people's access to the latest and most effective drugs. Euphemistically called the National Institute for Health and Clinical

---

A&E Patients Left in Ambulances for Up to Five Hours 'so trusts can meet government targets'

"Seriously ill patients are being kept in ambulances outside hospitals for hours so National Health Service trusts do not miss Government targets. Thousands of people a year are having to wait outside accident and emergency departments because trusts will not let them in until they can treat them within four hours, in line with a Labour pledge. The hold-ups mean ambulances are not available to answer fresh 999 calls. Doctors warned last night that the practice of 'patient-stacking' was putting patients' health at risk. Figures obtained by the Liberal Democrats show that last year 43,576 patients waited longer than one hour before being let into emergency units....Liberal Democrat health spokesman Norman Lamb is writing to health secretary Alan Johnson to demand an urgent investigation in the practice....'This is evidence of shocking systematic failure in our emergency services,' he said."

—Daniel Martin, *The Daily Mail* (London).[25]

Effectiveness (NICE), the agency determines which treatments the British health care system covers.

In early 2008, NICE refused to approve Abatacept, an arthritis drug sold in the United States under the brand-name Orencia. Even though it is one of a very few drugs clinically proven to improve severe rheumatoid arthritis, NICE magnanimously decided that "Abatacept could not be considered a cost effective use of [National Health Service] resources."[26]

In 2008, NICE made a similar decision about the lung cancer drug Tarceva. Despite numerous studies showing that the drug significantly prolongs the life of cancer patients—and the unanimous endorsement of lung cancer specialists throughout the U.K.—

NICE determined that the drug was too expensive to cover. As of August 2008, England is currently one of only three countries in Western Europe that deny citizens access to Tarceva.[27]

These are by no means exceptions, but more like the rule. In 2001, NICE concluded that Gleevec, a molecularly-targeted medicine, didn't treat leukemia more effectively than its older counterparts. At that time in the United States, people with leukemia were welcoming this new miracle drug. It took about two years for the British government to change its mind.[28]

In 2002, Americans with a rare stomach cancer started taking Gleevec because it was found to target and kill cancer cells without attacking healthy cells. It took almost a full two years after U.S. approval for Britain's clinical drug review agency to approve Gleevec's use for those with the cancer.[29]

Britain's behavior is typical—every European government rations drugs to save money. Eighty-five new drugs hit U.S. pharmacy shelves between 1998 and 2002. During that same time period, however, only 44 of those drugs were launched in Europe.[30]

European governments also control costs by paying doctors far less than what they would earn in a free market. On average, U.S. physicians take home close to $300,000 each year. However in Italy the average doctor earns $81,414. In Germany, the average physician salary drops to just $56,455,[31] and in France the salary is $55,000.[32]

As Swedish policy expert Johnny Munkhammar once explained, "European governments haven't figured out a way to deliver health care for less money—they've simply figured out a way to ration care."[33]

But what about outcomes?

So socialized medicine can't offer a paradise of free medical care. But aren't outcomes and big trends—like life expectancy and infant mortality—what matter? And in that respect, doesn't the United States lag far behind other advanced nations?

Not if one takes a hard look at the statistics.

In 2006, U.S. life expectancy reached a record high of 78.1 years.[34] Good news, to be sure. But that record number still put the nation behind almost 30 other countries. In Japan, Hong Kong, Canada, France, Sweden, and elsewhere, people are expected to live well past their 80th birthday.

Outcomes do matter. But the United States has nothing to be embarrassed about. Crude indicators like life expectancy and infant mortality don't reflect just reflect the quality of a health care system. They also reflect cultural, behavioral, and other factors, such as a nation's homicide rate, the number of accidents, diet trends, ethnic diversity, pre-natal habits and much more.

It's not pretty but it affects health care statistics. According to the U.S. Department of Justice, America's homicide rate was 5.9 per 100,000 inhabitants in 2004.[35] In contrast, it was 1.95 in Canada, 1.64 in France, and 0.98 in Germany.[36]

The United States also has more car accidents. According to the Department of Transportation, America had 14.24 fatalities per 100,000 people from auto accidents in 2006.[37] In Canada, the number was 9.25. In France, 7.4. In Germany, despite the country's high-speed autobahns, fatalities stood at just 6.19 per 100,000.[38]

Indeed, Robert Ohsfeldt of Texas A&M University and John Schneider of the University of Iowa recently concluded that Americans who don't die from homicides or in car accidents outlive people in every other Western country.[39]

As Harvard economist Greg Mankiw has noted, "Maybe these differences have lessons for traffic laws and gun control, but they teach us nothing about our system of health care."[40]

Similarly, infant mortality tells us less about the quality of a nation's health care system than one might think.

The World Health Organization defines a live birth as any infant that, once removed from its mother, "breathes or shows any other evidence of life such as beating of the heart, pulsation of the umbilical cord, or definite movement of voluntary muscles."[41] The United States follows that definition—counting the births of all citizens that show any sign of life, regardless of birth weight or prematurity.

Other nations are far more conservative. In France, for instance, the government requires a "medical certificate stating that the child was born alive and viable" in order to attest the death of a baby.[42] In Switzerland, "an infant must be at least 30 centimeters long at birth to be counted as living."[43] In France and Belgium, babies born at less than 26 weeks are automatically registered as dead.[44]

Plus, the United States has very sophisticated (and very expensive) neo-natal units. These help doctors keep premature babies alive, but such babies are at extremely high risk.

As for the WHO's look at overall health system performance—which ranked the United States 37th out of 191 countries—that research too is seriously flawed. For one thing, it used only life expectancy in assessing overall population health.[45] And that factor alone accounted for 25 percent of how the nation's health care system was ranked.[46]

Another factor accounting for 25 percent of a nation's ranking was "distribution of health," or fairness.[47] By this logic, treating everyone exactly the same is more important than treating people well. So long as everyone is equal—even if they're equally miserable—a nation will do quite well in the WHO ranking.

Calgary's quads: Born in the U.S.A.

"A rare set of identical quadruplets, born…to a Calgary woman at a Montana hospital, are in good health….The naturally conceived baby quads— Autumn, Brooke, Calissa, and Dahlia—were delivered by caesarean section Sunday in Great Falls….Their mother, Calgarian Karen Jepp, was transferred to Benefits Hospital in Montana last week when she began showing signs of going into labour, and no Canadian hospital had enough neonatal intensive-care beds for all four babies."

—Michelle Lang, *Calgary Herald*.[48]

How to measure a health system

In measuring the quality of a health care system, what really matters is how well it serves those who are sick. And it's here that America really excels.

Today, the United States leads the world in treating cancer.[49] With breast cancer, for instance, the survival rate after five years among American women is 83.9 percent. For women in Britain, it's just 69.7 percent. For men with prostate cancer, the survival rate is 91.9 percent here, yet 73.7 percent in France, and 51.1 percent in Britain. American men and women are more than 35 percent more likely to survive colon cancer than their British counterparts.[50]

Much of this success is due to cancer screening, in which the United States leads the world. For prostate cancer, American men regularly receive the Prostate-Specific Antigen test. For colon cancer, colonoscopies are regularly administered at age 50. American women regularly receive mammograms and MRIs for breast cancer, and for cervical cancer, women regularly receive Pap smears. There is a relatively new test for ovarian cancer that is very important, particularly where there is a history of ovarian cancer in the family.

As for the supposed cost advantage of universal health care? That's an illusion, too. True, other developed nations may spend less as a percentage of GDP than the United States on health care—but so does Sudan. Without considering *value*, such statistical acrobatics are worthless.

America leads the way

There's another reason health care costs more in America. And it's not just because we are a very wealthy nation, demanding the most expensive treatments, technology, and drugs. We're also investing more in medical research. Other countries are nowhere close.

Today, the United States is far and away the world's leader in medical research and development. America produces more than half of the $175 billion of health care technology products purchased globally.[51] And U.S. governmental outlays on medical research also dramatically outpace those of other nations.

In 2004, the federal government funded medical research to the tune of $18.4 billion. By contrast the European Union—which has a significantly larger population than the United States — allocated funds equal to just $3.7 billion for medical research.[52]

Further, the gap in output and sales between the United States and other countries is stunning. Between 1999 and 2005, the U.S. was responsible for 71 percent of the sales of new pharmaceuticals. The next two largest pharmaceutical markets—Japan and Germany—account for just four percent each.[53]

Other nations deal with the "problem" of high medical costs by simply imposing price controls, refusing to pay an amount that reflects the true costs of innovation. Needless to say, such controls cut deeply into the incentives for innovation within those countries. But they also reduce revenue flows to American firms that have done—and continue to do—the expensive and very risky research. As a result, U.S. firms find themselves strapped for resources as they search for the breakthroughs that everyone around the world welcomes and uses.

The U.S. market for medical innovation is robust. Americans for the most part get cutting-edge care because we demand it, can afford it, and are willing to pay for it. Those miraculous advances may be costly, but as we've seen, they add life value. We get what we pay for.

While no one can deny that there are significant problems in the American health care system, overall it provides exceptional value. From the broad perspective, our health care is not a drag on us but a boon to the quality of our lives. After all, why do so many people from other nations come here for treatment?

When Italian Prime Minister Silvio Berlusconi needed heart surgery in 2006, for example, he traveled to the Cleveland Clinic—widely considered America's best hospital for cardiac care. So much for the "free" health care he could have received in Italy, or for that matter in London or Paris, the cities Michael Moore featured in his movie *Sicko*. If European health care was so great, why did Berlusconi come to the United States? Similarly, as mentioned earlier in this chapter, when Canadian parliament member Belinda Stronach needed breast cancer treatment in 2007, she headed to a California hospital.

NHS Threat to halt Care for Cancer Patient

"Colette Mills, a former nurse, has been told that if she attempts to top up her treatment privately, she will have to foot the entire £10,000 bill for drugs and care. The bizarre threat stems from the refusal by the government to let patients pay for additional drugs that are not prescribed by the National Health Service. Ministers say it is unfair on patients who cannot afford such top-up drugs and that it will create a two-tier NHS. It is thought thousands of patients suffer as a result of the policy. Mills, 58, is thought to be the first to take a public stand in challenging her NHS trust to allow her to pay for the drug as part of her NHS treatment. She wants to top up her treatment with Avastin. 'The policy of my local NHS trust is that I must be an NHS patient or a private patient,' she said. 'If I want to pay for Avastin, I must pay for everything. It's immoral that the drugs are out there and freely available to certain people, yet they say I cannot have it.'" With many 'wonder drugs' in the pipeline that the NHS is unlikely to fund, her predicament is likely to be shared by increasing numbers of patients who could afford additional life-extending drugs but not at the cost of their entire care."

—Sarah-Kate Templeton, *The Sunday Times*.[54]

Turning toward a freer market

The U.S. government already pays for more than half the nation's health care expenses. As lawmakers contemplate expanding that slice of the pie, it's worth noting that some European and Canadian leaders are pushing for their nations to *reduce* the government's role.

Take Claude Castonguay, called the "father of Quebec Medicare." Back in 1966, Quebec's premier asked Castonguay to head a royal commission to study health reform. At the commission's conclusion, Castonguay recommended that Quebec adopt a public health insurance system.[55]

The Quebec government followed his advice. By 1972, each province had established its own system of free access to doctors' services, which the federal government helped fund.[56]

Several decades later, in March 2007, the Quebec government once again asked Castonguay to lead a health reform task force —this time looking into new ways to finance the system.[57] In February 2008, Castonguay concluded that the system is in "crisis," and called for the private sector to play a greater role.

In Britain, too, lawmakers are realizing that without unlimited funding, it's not possible to dole out an adequate supply of health care services. Not even close.

Historically, the private sector played but a small role in Britain's health system. Those with the money purchased their own insurance or simply paid cash to doctors to jump the line when they needed treatment. Today, however, the government is looking toward private sector providers to save the NHS as the system's finances are essentially spiraling out of control.[58]

Solutions: Markets, Consumer Choice, and Innovation

None of the preceding chapters is meant to suggest that America's health care system is perfect. It's not. Costs are high, and too many Americans get left behind. Reform is desperately needed.

But true reform of the health care system requires less government interference—not more. Only with a freer market can we lower costs and achieve quality universal health care. If we have universal choice in health care, we will reach universal coverage —a goal supported by all of us.

Consider Lasik corrective eye surgery. Because most insurance providers including government programs won't cover the procedure, the market isn't distorted by excessive regulations. Providers operate in a free market where technology is constantly advancing, price competition is fierce, and the consumer is king. Companies rise and fall according to their ability to provide customer satisfaction.

In the past decade, more than three million Lasik procedures have been performed. During that time, the average price of Lasik eye surgery has dropped nearly 40 percent, from $2,200 to $1,350 per eye.

Unfortunately, Lasik is a rare exception to the general rule. In just about every other area of health care, the government is heavily involved. So the key to lowering costs and expanding coverage is to expand the Lasik model. That means encouraging competition by decreasing government's role in the health care marketplace.

Here are a few commonsense ideas to lead us to affordable, high quality, accessible health care:

Change the Tax Code

Few people expect their employers to provide food, housing, or life insurance. Yet because of a historical accident, people do expect their employers to provide health care. Today, more than 60 percent of those under age 65 are covered by a health insurance policy paid for in full or partially by an employer.[1]

During World War II, wage controls prevented employers from rewarding workers with salary hikes and enticing new workers with cash. So companies started offering health care benefits as a way around the law.

Employers viewed this outlay as a business expense, paying for the benefits with pre-tax dollars. At first, the IRS complained. But soon, the federal government changed the tax code and employer-provided health care became the status quo. Today, we have a system of pre-paid medical care. As a result, employees don't think about the real cost of going to a doctor and receiving treatment.

Over the years, this has handicapped the nation's economy.

For starters, employer-provided coverage makes it harder for people to leave their jobs—because they're afraid they'll lose their insurance on top of their paychecks. That, in turn, reduces competition between employers seeking to attract talented workers, thus reducing wages.

It also stifles new business creation, as many folks are unwilling to forego health insurance to pursue entrepreneurial ventures—especially if they have a chronic or pre-existing medical condition.

Also, because workers don't directly pay for their own health care, they often lack a clear understanding of how much their coverage actually costs. They tend to think they're getting health insurance for free. In fact, it isn't free at all. They're just paying for it indirectly in the form of smaller paychecks.

The effect of this disconnect is insidious. Because employees think they're getting free coverage, they don't shop around for the best deal. They just take whatever plan their employers offer them. As a result, people wind up with coverage that's in their employer's best interest, not theirs. Meanwhile, insurance providers are insulated from normal market pressures to keep customers happy and prices low.

This system is also unfair because it penalizes the unemployed and individuals, who cannot purchase health insurance with pre-tax dollars.

Fortunately, this is an easy problem to solve. Simply give individuals that same tax break that companies already receive when buying health coverage. Such a change would level the playing field.

There are two ideas being discussed to do this.

Under one plan, the tax code would be reformed to provide refundable tax credits—$2,500 for individuals and $5,000 for families.

The second plan would change the tax code to allow income tax deductions for health care expenditures—$7,500 for individuals and $15,000 for families.

Either change would essentially give all Americans the same tax benefits already enjoyed by those with employer-based insurance. And either one would completely transform the health care market. There would be no more confusion about how much insurance costs. The disconnect between provider and consumer would disappear, resulting in lower prices and higher customer satisfaction. Workers could purchase their own insurance tax-free, and wouldn't have to worry about losing coverage between jobs. Best of all, individuals could choose the insurance package best suited to their needs, as opposed to their employer's needs.

Reduce costly government mandates and regulations

Earlier in this book, I explained how excessive state mandates and regulations—like "guaranteed issue" and "community rating" —drive up the cost of health care. According to the Council for Affordable Health Insurance, mandated benefits can increase the cost of health insurance by up to 50 percent.[2]

Some mandates are defensible, of course, but most aren't. Providers shouldn't be required to cover treatments like massage therapy, breast reduction, in-vitro fertilization, and hair prosthesis. These are hardly critical components of a good health insurance policy. But they add tremendously to the cost of coverage.

Removing needless mandates from insurance policies in the states might not grab headlines, but such a strategy would be extremely effective in terms of expanding coverage and lowering costs.

Allow the purchase of insurance across state lines

State borders act as regulatory walls, denying Americans access to health insurance plans in other states. Because state regulations vary so widely, a standard insurance policy in one state can be more than five times more expensive than a standard policy in another state.

Take the case of a hypothetical 25-year-old man from New Jersey. According to the Commonwealth Fund, he would have to shell out roughly $5,580 each year for a standard health insurance policy. A similar policy in Kentucky—which has far fewer mandated coverage benefits than New Jersey—would run him just $960 annually.

So if our 25-year old were allowed to purchase a policy across state lines, he could save more than $4,600 per year and would be more likely to purchase coverage than go without.

Just by letting people shop around for the best value in the insurance marketplace, we could dramatically lower costs, while expanding the number of options available to consumers. Interstate shopping would also create competition among providers from different states, which would drive costs down even further.

Expand Health Savings Accounts

Lawmakers should also work to make Health Savings Accounts (HSAs) more attractive by reducing regulations on them.

An HSA is a tax-free, interest-accruing savings account that can be used to pay for routine medical expenses. It is purchased in tandem with an inexpensive, qualified, high-deductible insurance policy designed to cover major health care costs. HSA holders can spend their money tax-free on health care as they see fit, without asking their insurance providers for permission.

If someone is generally healthy, the HSA funds build up over time —and can eventually work just like a retirement savings plan. (When an HSA holder reaches 65 or is disabled, the money can be withdrawn without a penalty for non-healthcare expenses. One just needs to pay income tax on the withdrawal.) HSAs don't disappear when a person is between jobs. And when a person is faced with an extremely expensive health emergency, the insurance policy kicks in—and the HSA simply covers the deductible.

These plans put the "insurance" back into health insurance. Since their creation in 2003 and implementation in January 2004, HSAs have already made insurance more affordable, while giving people control over their health care dollars. Today, more than six million Americans have HSA-compatible health insurance plans.[3]

As of 2008, individuals are allowed to contribute up to $2,900 each year to their HSAs. Families are allowed to sock away up to $5,800. By raising this limit and reducing some restrictions like the size of the highest allowable deductible, Congress would make HSAs even more appealing.

Support retail health clinics

Until a few years ago, if you needed medicine for a sore throat or an earache, you had to schedule a trip to the doctor's office. If you happened to get sick after business hours or during the weekend, or had no insurance, too bad—unless, of course, you were willing to wait for hours in an emergency room.

These days, however, there are other options. Across the country, retail health clinics are sprouting up in large stores like Wal-Mart and Target, as well as pharmacies like CVS. Patients generally don't need an appointment to visit these clinics. And they don't have to wait more than a few minutes for treatment.

Retail clinics typically charge around $50 per visit, and are generally open 24/7. If patients are prescribed a drug, they can often fill the prescription right there.[4] This is the ultimate in price transparency.

These clinics have also proven quite effective at helping the uninsured access medical treatment. A 2007 Harris Interactive poll found that 22 percent of clinic visitors were uninsured. Wal-Mart claims that around half its clinic customers are uninsured.[5]

In response to consumer demand, retail companies are already reforming our health care system by setting up clinics that provide affordable medical care around the clock, regardless of whether you have insurance or not. By the end of 2008, it's estimated that there will be around 2,000 retail health clinics.[6]

Unfortunately, not everyone sees this as good news.

Many doctors are asking the American Medical Association to urge federal lawmakers to ban these clinics.[7] Although these doctors claim that patient safety is their concern, it's quite obvious that they're actually seeking to restrict competition in order to protect their incomes. Lawmakers should support the growth of retail health clinics by resisting calls to protect doctors from lower-priced competition.

In some states, lawmakers are pushing for the government to mandate a low nurse practitioner to doctor ratio. Such a move would simply increase costs and reduce the incentives to establish retail clinics in those states.

Implement tort reform

Any meaningful health care reform must bring malpractice lawsuits under control, as the U.S. litigation system is costing patients dearly.

Each year, one out of eight physicians gets hit with a medical malpractice lawsuit. Malpractice insurance can cost specialty physicians as much as $240,000 per year, and is driving doctors out of specialties like obstetrics and neurosurgery. Plus, liability concerns prompt physicians to practice defensive medicine, ordering more procedures and tests than they would otherwise, hence adding to the increased health care costs.

According to a study by Lawrence McQuillan and Hovannes Abramyan of the Pacific Research Institute, this drains $124 billion from America's health care system, adding 3.4 million Americans to the rolls of the uninsured.

Policymakers must put an end to the lawsuit lottery. Sensible reforms include capping non-economic damage awards such as in California under its MICRA law and in Texas, allowing defendants to pay large awards in periodic payments, moving to a system of binding arbitration, and placing reasonable limits on attorneys' fees.

Such reforms would significantly reduce hidden litigation costs and help prevent a shortage of medical specialists in states with expensive medical malpractice insurance.

Provide vouchers for the working poor and chronically uninsured

Simply reducing regulations and taking a free-market approach won't solve all our health care problems. Such an approach would still leave behind those who do not have employer-provided coverage but are the chronically ill, those who earn too little to afford private insurance but too much to qualify for welfare, or our veterans who deserve better care than what they may be getting now.

For these folks, lawmakers should create a system of insurance vouchers, similar to the school vouchers conceptualized by Nobel Prize-winning economist Milton Friedman. With health vouchers, the chronically ill and working poor could purchase insurance from a private company or through a high-risk state pool.

Any free-market reform of our health care system needs to address the fact that some people will fall through the cracks—even if insurance is made dramatically more affordable. By providing vouchers, government can ensure that everyone has insurance, without bogging down the health care market in a quagmire of red tape.

Starkly different choices

Virtually everyone agrees that America's health care system is in dire need of reform. But how do we fix it?

In the political debate today, we face a stark choice. We can let the government take over and try to solve the problem by reducing our options, imposing mandates, raising taxes, and distorting the open market. Or we can put doctors, patients, and consumers in charge by liberating the health care market, maximizing choice, and spurring innovation.

It is my sincere hope that this book has convinced you that the American health care system needs more freedom—not more government. As P.J. O'Rourke says, "If you think health care is expensive now, just wait until it's free."

Endnotes

Introduction

[1] "Facts on Health Care Costs," National Coalition on Health Care, Washington, D.C., 2008, http://www.nchc.org/facts/cost_fact_sheet_2008.pdf

[2] Ibid.

[3] Robin Toner and Janet Elder; Megan Thee, Marina Stefan and Marjorie Connelly contributed reporting, "Most Support U.S. Guarantee of Health Care," *New York Times*, March 02, 2007, http://query.nytimes.com/gst/fullpage.html?res=9e06e7d71631f931a35750c0a9619c8b63&sec=health&spon=&pagewanted=2; "Government Should Make Sure All Have Health Care, U.S. Voters Tell Quinnipiac University National Poll; Sen. Clinton Seen as Leader on Health Issue," Quinnipiac University, Hamden, CT, November 1, 2007, http://www.quinnipiac.edu/x1295.xml?ReleaseID=1114; "Poll: Public Supports Health Care for All," *USA Today*, October 19, 2003, http://www.usatoday.com/news/health/2003-10-19-health-poll_x.htm.

[4] Jeffrey M. Jones, "Majority of Americans Satisfied with Their Healthcare Plans," Gallup, November 29, 2007, http://www.gallup.com/poll/102934/Majority-Americans-Satisfied-Their-Own-Healthcare.aspx; "Poll: The Politics of Health Care," *CBS News*, March 1, 2007, http://www.cbsnews.com/stories/2007/03/01/opinion/polls/main2528357.shtml

[5] "Obama Takes an Early Commanding Lead Over McCain," National Political Issues Survey, *L.A. Times*/Bloomberg Poll, June 24, 2008, http://www.calendarlive.com/media/acrobat/2008-06/40351172.pdf

Myth One

1 "Cancer Survival in Five Continents: A worldwide population based study (Concord)," *Lancet Oncology*, Vol. 9, August 2008.

2 Robert Samuelson, *RealClearPolitics.com*, September 10, 2008.

3 Victoria Craig Bunce and J.P. Wieske, "Health Insurance Mandates in the States 2008," Council of Affordable Health Insurance, http://www.cahi.org/cahi_contents/resources/pdf/HealthInsuranceMandates2008.pdf

4 Board of Trustees, Federal Hospital Insurance and Federal Supplementary Medical Insurance Trust Funds, Annual Report, 2008. http://www.cms.hhs.gov/ReportsTrustFunds/downloads/tr2008.pdf

5 PriceWaterhouseCoopers, "The Factors Fueling Rising Healthcare Costs," 2006, http://www.ahip.org/redirect/PwC-CostOfHC2006.pdf

6 Benjamin Zycher, "Comparing Public and Private Health Insurance: Would A Single-Payer System Save Enough to Cover the Uninsured?" *Medical Progress Report*, No. 5, October 2007.

7 Milt Freudenheim, "Low Payments by U.S. Raise Medical Bills Billions a Year," *New York Times*, June 1, 2006, http://www.nytimes.com/2006/06/01/business/01health.html?_r=2&oref=slogin&pagewanted=print&oref=login

8 Daniel P. Kessler, "Cost Shifting in California Hospitals: What is the Effect on Private Payers?" (Sacramento, California: California Foundation for Commerce and Education, June 6, 2007), http://www.cfcepolicy.org/NR/rdonlyres/46C2B526-D9BF-4556-A310-37C3A7CDF53D/30/CFCE_Cost_Shift_Study.pdf

9 "Diocletian and the House of Constantine," *The Encyclopedia of World History: Ancient, Medieval, and Modern, Chronologically Arranged*, 6th Edition, Peter N. Stearns, general editor, (Boston, Massachusetts: Houghton Mifflin Company, 2001), http://www.bartleby.com/67/261.html

10 Joseph A. DiMasi and Henry G. Grabowski, "The Cost of Biopharmaceutical R&D: Is Biotech Different?" *Managerial and Decision Economics*, 28 (2007): 469-479. (Cited in PhRMA's *Profile 2008, Pharmaceutical Industry*.[PhRMA])

11 Sean Keehan, Andrea Sisko, Christopher Truffer, Sheila Smith, Cathy Cowan, John Poisal, M. Kent Clemens, the National Health Expenditure Accounts Projections Team, "Health Spending Projections Through 2017: The Baby-Boom Generation Is Coming to Medicare," *Health Affairs*, February 26, 2008, http://content.healthaffairs.org/cgi/reprint/27/2/w145

12 *Tracking the Care of Patients with Severe Chronic Illness: The Dartmouth Atlas of Health Care 2008*, Dartmouth Atlas Project, (Lebanon, NH: Dartmouth Institute for Health Policy & Clinical Practice, April, 2008).

13 Sean Keehan, Andrea Sisko, Christopher Truffer, Sheila Smith, Cathy Cowan, John Poisal, M. Kent Clemens, the National Health Expenditure Accounts Projections Team, "Health Spending Projections Through 2017: The Baby-Boom Generation Is Coming to Medicare," *Health Affairs*.

14 Clifford J. Levy and Michael Luo, "New York Medicaid Fraud May Reach into Billions," *New York Times*, July 18, 2005.

15 Ibid.

16 Cited in Martha M. Hamilton, "On Medicare and Scorned by the Docs," *The Washington Post*, April 6, 2008.

17 Ibid.

18 Mark V. Pauly, "Markets Without Magic: How Competition Might Save Medicare," American Enterprise Institute, April 4, 2001.

19 Vanessa Fuhrmans, "Note to Medicaid Patients: The Doctor Won't See You," *The Wall Street Journal*, June 19, 2007.

20 Doug Trapp, "Senate panel OKs SCHIP funding bill; Bush threatens to veto it," AMNews, The American Medical Association, August 6, 2007, http://www.ama-assn.org/amednews/2007/08/06/gvsb0806.htm; Fannie Chen, Usha Ranji, and Alina Salganicoff "Children's Coverage and SCHIP Reauthorization," Background Brief, Kaiser Family Foundation, (Menlo Park, CA, May, 2007), http://www.kaiseredu.org/topics_im.asp?id=704&imID=1&parentID=65

21 Benjamin Brewer, "Hassles Force a Retreat from Military Families," *The Wall Street Journal*, May 8, 2008.

Myth Two

1   David Gratzer, *The Cure: How Capitalism Can Save American Health Care*, New York, New York, Encounter Books, 2006.

2   Robert E. Hall and Charles I. Jones, "The Value of Life and the Rise in Health Spending," *The Quarterly Journal of Economics*, MIT Press, 122, no. 1 (February 2007), 39-72.

3   Centers for Medicare and Medicaid Factsheet, http://www.cms.hhs.gov/NationalHealthExpendData/25_NHE_Fact_Sheet.asp#TopOfPage

4   Conversation with Chad Wilkinson, July 29, 2008.

5   David Gratzer, *The Cure*.

6   Vanessa Fuhrmans, "Medical Specialties Hit by a Growing Pay Gap," *The Wall Street Journal*, May 5, 2007, p. A1.

7   http://www.econ.yale.edu/seminars/labor/lap04-05/topel032505.pdf

8   David Gratzer, *The Cure*.

9   Mary Carter, "Heart disease still the most likely reason you'll die," CNN.com, November 1, 2006.

10 Kevin M. Murphy and Robert H. Topel , "The Value of Health and Longevity," Milken Foundation, Lasker Charitable Trust, and the Stigler Center, March 15, 2005, http://www.econ.yale.edu/seminars/labor/lap04-05/topel032505.pdf

11 Central Intelligence Agency, *2008 World Fact Book*, https://www.cia.gov/library/publications/the-world-factbook/covers/cover-2008front.html

12 Murphy and Topel, "The Value of Health and Longevity."

13 Kevin M. Murphy and Robert Topel Eds, "The Economic Value of Medical Research," *Measuring the Gains from Medical Research: An Economic Approach*, ed. Murphy and Topel, Chicago, Illinois, University of Chicago Press, 2002.

14 Greg Scandlen, "Making Americans Care about Health Care Spending," The Reason Foundation, January 24, 2007, http://www.reason.org/commentaries/scandlen_20070124.shtml

15 Robert E. Hall and Charles I. Jones, "The Value of Life and the Rise in Health Spending," *The Quarterly Journal of Economics*, MIT Press, February 2007. Older version here: http://economics.uchicago.edu/download/hx200.pdf

16 Ibid.
17 Ibid.

Myth Three

1   http://www.barackobama.com/issues/healthcarehealth care/
2   On Sept 24, 2008, a search for the term "46 million uninsured" in quotation marks resulted in "about 25,000" hits on Google.
3   http://en.wikipedia.org/wiki/Uninsured (September 11, 2008)
4   Population estimate as of July, 2008, "Canada," *The 2008 World Factbook*, (Washington DC: Central Intelligence Agency, 2008), https://www.cia.gov/library/publications/the-world-factbook/print/ca.html
5   Carmen DeNavas-Walt, Bernadette D. Proctor, and Jessica Smith, *Income, Poverty, and Health Insurance Coverage in the United States: 2006*, (Washington, DC: U.S. Census Bureau, 2007), http://www.census.gov/prod/2007pubs/p60-233.pdf, p.57.
6   Ibid.
7   Ibid. p. 21
8   Jack Hadley, John Holahan, Teresa Conghlin and Dawn Miller, "Covering the Uninsured in 2008: Current Costs, Sources of Payment, and Incremental Costs," *Health Affairs*, 27, No. 5, August 25, 2008.
9   Jennifer L. Kriss, Sara R. Collins, Bisundev Mahato, Elise Gould, and Cathy Schoen, "Rite of Passage? Why Young Adults Become Uninsured and How New Policies Can Help, 2008 Update," (New York: Commonwealth Fund, May, 2008), http://www.commonwealthfund.org/usr_doc/Kriss_riteofpassage2008_1139_ib.pdf?section=4039
10 Laura Vanderkam, "Health insurance doesn't have to hurt," *USA Today*, June 6, 2006.
11 Dick Morris and Eileen Mc Gann, "O's Health Rx: Cover Illegals," *New York Post*, July 21, 2008, http://www.nypost.com/seven/07212008/postopinion/opedcolumnists/os_health_rx__cover_illegals_120816.htm
12 "The Uninsured in America," (Chicago, Illinois: Blue Cross Blue Shield Association, February 27, 2003), http://www.coverageforall.org/pdf/BC-BS_Uninsured-America.pdf; John C. Goodman and

Devon M. Herrick, "The Case against John Kerry's Health Plan," (Dallas, Texas: National Center for Policy Analysis, September, 2004), http://www.ncpa.org/pub/st/st269/st269.pdf,

13   David Gratzer, "What Health Insurance Crisis?" *Los Angeles Times*, August 29, 2004, http://www.manhattan-institute.org/html/_latimes-what_health.htm

14   *Reaching Eligible but Uninsured Children in Medicaid and SCHIP*, (Washington DC: Georgetown University Health Policy Institute, Center for Children and Families, March, 2008), http://ccf.georgetown.edu/index/cms-filesystem-action?file=strategy+center%2Feligibleuninsured%2Feligibleuninsuredccf.pdf

15   http://www.barackobama.com/issues/healthcare/

16   "Medicaid-Eligible Adults Who Are Not Enrolled: Who Are They and Do They Get the Care They Need?" Urban Institute, Series A, No. A-48, October 2001, http://www.urban.org/publications/310378.html

17   Diana Manos, "Kennedy-Dingell bill would expand Medicare to all," *Healthcare Finance News*, April 27, 2007, http://www.healthcarefinancenews.com/story.cms?id=6405

18   BlueCross BlueShield Association, "BCBSA Analysis Shows One-third of Uninsured Americans Could Have Affordable, Quality Healthcare Coverage Immediately," May 9, 2003, http://www.bcbs.com/news/bcbsa/bcbsa-analysis-shows.html?templateName=template-28767547&print=t

19   Carmen DeNavas-Walt, Bernadette D. Proctor, and Jessica Smith, *Income, Poverty, and Health Insurance Coverage in the United States: 2006*, (Washington, DC: U.S. Census Bureau, 2007), p, 21, http://www.census.gov/prod/2007pubs/p60-233.pdf; Also see, "Health Insurance," Health Insurance Coverage (Reports and Tables), (Washington DC: U.S. Census Bureau, Housing and Household Economic Statistics Division), http://www.census.gov/hhes/www/hlthins/cps.html

20   Carmen DeNavas-Walt, Bernadette D. Proctor, and Jessica Smith, *Income, Poverty, and Health Insurance Coverage in the United States: 2006* p. 21.

Myth Four

[1] Gina Kolata and Andrew Pollack, "Costly Cancer Drug Offers Hope, but Also a Dilemma," *New York Times*, July 6, 2008, http://www.nytimes.com/2008/07/06/health/06avastin.html

[2] "Ireland," *The 2008 World Factbook*, (Washington DC: Central Intelligence Agency, 2008), https://www.cia.gov/library/publications/the-world-factbook/geos/ei.html#Econ

[3] (Total number of households = 111,162,259. 286,500,000,000/111,162,259=2 577.31358), "TABLE 1. Projections of Households by Type: 1995 to 2010, Series 1, 2, and 3," *U.S. Population Projections* (Washington DC: U.S. Census Bureau, May, 1996), http://www.census.gov/population/projections/nation/hh-fam/table1n.txt

[4] http://finance.google.com/finance?q=NYSE:PFE

[5] "Lipitor," Drugstore.com, http://www.drugstore.com/pharmacy/prices/drugprice.asp?ndc=00071015534&trx=1Z5006

[6] Kolata and Pollack, "Costly Cancer Drug Offers Hope."

[7] (2006 Median Household Income = $48,451), Bruce H. Webster Jr. and Alemayehu Bishaw, *Income, Earnings, and Poverty Data From the 2006 American Community Survey*, (Washington DC: U.S. Census Bureau, August 2007), http://www.census.gov/prod/2007pubs/acs-08.pdf.

[8] John R. Graham, "Squeezing the Balloon: The Futility of Pharmaceutical Cost Containment," *Health Policy Prescriptions*, 4 no. 6, (San Francisco, California: Pacific Research Institute, June 2006) http://special.pacificresearch.org/pub/hpp/2006/hpp_06-06.html

[9] Gerard Anderson, *Chronic Conditions: Making the Case for Ongoing Care*, (Baltimore, Maryland: Partnership Solutions and Johns Hopkins University, November 2007). (Cited in PhRMA's *Profile 2008, Pharmaceutical Industry*.) http://www.fightchronicdisease.com/news/pfcd/documents/ChronicCareChartbook_FINAL.pdf

[10] Kenneth E. Thorpe, Curtis S. Florence, and Peter Joski, "Which Medical Conditions Account for the Rise in Health Care Spending?" *Health Affairs* Web Exclusive, August 25, 2004): W4-437--W4-445. (Cited in PhRMA's *Profile 2008, Pharmaceutical Industry*.)

11 "Most American Adults Have at Least One Chronic Medical Condition," *News and Numbers*, Agency for Healthcare Research and Quality, May 28, 2008. http://www.ahrq.gov/news/nn/nn052808.htm

12 Sally C. Pipes, "Brave New Diet," *The Washington Post*, December 26, 2007, http://www.washingtonpost.com/wp-dyn/content/article/2007/12/25/AR2007122500862.html

13 "Statistics Related to Overweight and Obesity," Weight-Control Information Network, May, 2007, http://win.niddk.nih.gov/statistics/

14 "Statistics on the Aging Population," Administration on Aging, Department of Health Services, http://www.aoa.dhhs.gov/prof/Statistics/statistics.aspx

15 "State-specific Estimates of Diagnosed Diabetes Among Adults, Age-Adjusted Prevalence of Diagnosed Diabetes per 100 Adult Population, by State, United States, 1994 and 2004," *Data & Trends, National Diabetes Surveillance System*, (Washington DC: Centers for Disease Control and Prevention), http://www.cdc.gov/diabetes/statistics/prev/state/fPrev1994and2004.htm

16 "Blood Pressure Rates On Rise Again on U.S.," *New York Times*, August 24, 2004, http://query.nytimes.com/gst/fullpage.html?res=9E01E5DA143EF937A1575BC0A9629C8B63

17 Miranda Hitti, "Heart Disease Kills Every 34 Seconds in U.S.," FOX News, December 27, 2004, http://www.foxnews.com/story/0,2933,142436,00.html

18 Anderson, *Chronic Conditions*. http://www.fightchronicdisease.com/news/pfcd/documents/ChronicCareChartbook_FINAL.pdf

19 Ibid.

20 Eric U. Luy, "Untreated Diabetes Exposes Patients to Future Complications." Healthlink, Medical College of Wisconsin, http://healthlink.mcw.edu/article/949089492.html

21 Keith A. Fox, *et al.* "Decline in Rates of Death and Heart Failure in Acute Coronary Syndromes, 1999-2006," *Journal of the American Medical Association*, 297 (2007): 17, 1892-1900. http://www.phrma.org/index.php?Itemid=89&id=944&option=com_content&task=view

22 Ibid.

23 M.C. Sokol et al., "Impact of Medication Adherence on Hospitaliza-tion Risk and Healthcare Cost," *Medical Care*, 43, no. 6 (June 2005), 521-530. (Cited in PhRMA's Profile 2008, *Pharmaceutical Industry*.)

24 Baoping Shang, and Dana P. Goldman, "Prescription Drug Cover-age and Elderly Medicare Spending," National Bureau of Economic Research, *Working Paper 13358*, September, 2007, http://www.nber.org/papers/w13358

25 PhRMA, based on data from Tufts University, Tufts Center for the Study of Drug Development (1995). As cited in PhRMA's *Profile 2008, Pharmaceutical Industry.*

26 Sally C. Pipes, "Under proposed changes to U.S. patent law, com-ing up with a new, life-saving drug may not be worth it," *The Star Tribune* (Minneapolis-St. Paul), March 6, 2008, http://www.startri-bune.com/opinion/commentary/16364136.html

27 Joseph A. DiMasi, and Henry G. Grabowski, "The Cost of Biophar-maceutical R&D: Is Biotech Different?" *Managerial and Decision Economics*, 28, 2007, pp, 469-479. (Cited in PhRMA's *Profile 2008, Pharmaceutical Industry*.)

28 J. Vernon, J. Golec, and J. DiMasi, "Drug Development Costs when Financial Risk is Measured Using the Fama-French Three Factor Model," unpublished working paper, January 2008. (Cited in PhRMA's *Profile 2008, Pharmaceutical Industry*.)

29 Sally C. Pipes, "Under proposed changes to U.S. patent law…"

30 Shelley Wood, "Average U.S. Total–Cholesterol Levels Fall Below 200mg/dl," HeartWire, December 14, 2007.

31 David Brown, "Life Expectancy Hits Record High in United States," *The Washington Post*, June 12, 2008, http://www.washingtonpost.com/wp-dyn/content/article/2008/06/11/AR2008061101570.html?hpid=sec-health

32 Frank R. Lichtenberg, "The Expanding Pharmaceutical Arsenal in the War on Cancer," National Bureau of Economic Research Working Paper no. 10328 (Cambridge, MA: NBER, February 2004). (Cited in PhRMA's *Profile 2008, Pharmaceutical Industry*.)

33 Sally C. Pipes, "Five myths of health care," *The Washington Times*, March 21, 2008, http://www.washingtontimes.com/news/2008/mar/21/five-myths-of-health-care/?page=2

34 *Adis R&D Insight Database*, 27 February 2008. As cited in PhRMA's *Profile 2008, Pharmaceutical Industry*. http://www.drugdiscoveryonline.com/Search.mvc?page=174&sort=Date%20ASC&keyword=Currentl y%2C%20there%20are%20more%20than%202%2C700%20new&se archType=2&override=Currently%2C%20there%20are%20more%2 0than%202%2C700%20new

35 John R. Graham, "Squeezing the Balloon."

36 Stephen Saul "Helped by Generics, Inflation of Drug Costs Slows, *New York Times*, September 21, 2007.

37 Sally C. Pipes, "A Primer for Follow-On Biologics," RealClear-Politics, June 6, 2008, http://www.realclearpolitics.com/articles/2008/06/a_primer_for_followon_biologic.html

38 Catherine Larkin, "Generics Capture 65% of U.S. Market as Costs Rise (Update 1)," *Bloomberg.com*, February 12, 2008, http://www.bloomberg.com/apps/news?pid=20601091&sid=a8ho28TjBN7M&refer=india

39 Marc Kaufman, "Generic Drugs Hit Backlog at FDA," *The Washington Post*, February 4, 2006, http://www.washingtonpost.com/wp-dyn/content/article/2006/02/03/AR2006020302598.html

40 Patricia Barry, "AARP Report: Generic Drug Prices Go Down Sharply," *AARP Bulletin Today*, May 15, 2008, http://bulletin.aarp.org/yourhealth/medications/articles/aarp_report__generic.html

41 Stephanie Saul, "Helped By Generics, Inflation of Drug Costs Slows," *New York Times*, September 21, 2007, http://www.nytimes.com/2007/09/21/business/21generic.html?ref=business

42 Sally C. Pipes, "Dems aim to railroad through bad bill on Medicare Part D," *The Hill*, January 9, 2007, http://thehill.com/op-eds/dems-aim-to-railroad-through-bad-bill-on-medicare-part-d-2007-01-09.html

43 Frank R. Lichtenberg, "Benefits and Costs of Newer Drugs: Evidence from the 1996 Medical Expenditure Panel Survey," National Bureau of Economic Research, *Working Paper 8147*, March 2001, http://papers.nber.org/papers/w8147

Myth Five

1 "Eighty Percent of U.S. Adults Favor Allowing Importation of Prescription Drugs," *The Wall Street Journal*/Harris Interactive Poll, Vol. 5, Issue 15, September 15, 2006.

[2] Jyoti Thottam, "Why Canada Won't Be Our Pharmacy," *Time*, November 14, 2004, http://www.time.com/time/magazine/article/0,9171,1101041122-782144,00.html?promoid=rss_nation

[3] Sally C. Pipes, "Cheaper Doesn't Mean Better. Ask a Canadian," *The Washington Post*, September 21, 2003.

[4] Henry G. Grabowski and Y. Richard Wang, "Trends; The Quantity And Quality Of Worldwide New Drug Introductions, 1982-2003; The United States has taken the lead worldwide in innovative performance and as a first-launch location for new drug introductions," *Health Affairs*, March 2006-April 2006. http://www.lexis.com/research/retrieve?_m=8903a350 389c429303aac75b7708da6d&_browseType=TEXTONLY&docnum=1 &_fmtstr=FULL&_startdoc=1&wchp=dGLbVzW-zSkAA&_md5=f826 b88d3cca6f2ea3de9b0e92243786

[5] PhRMA, based on data from Tufts University, Tufts Center for the Study of Drug Development (1995). As cited in PhRMA's *Profile 2008, Pharmaceutical Industry*.

[6] Pharmaceutical Research and Manufacturers of America, *Pharmaceutical Industry Profile 2008*, (Washington, DC: PhRMA, March 2008), http://www.phrma.org/files/2008%20Profile.pdf

[7] Robert Goldberg, "Don't Blame Canada," *National Review Online*, December 23, 2004, http://www.nationalreview.com/comment/goldberg200412230817.asp

[8] "HHS Task Force on Drug Importation," Report on Prescription Drug Importation, (Washington DC: Department of Health and Human Services, December, 2004), http://www.hhs.gov/importtaskforce/Report1220.pdf

[9] Elizabeth M. Whelan, "The Drug Importation Hoax," *National Review Online*, June 16, 2005, http://www.nationalreview.com/comment/whelan200506160741.asp

[10] Panos Kanavos and Paul Holmes, "Pharmaceutical Parallel Trade in the UK," (London: The Institute for the Study of Civil Society, April, 2005), http://www.civitas.org.uk/pdf/ParallelTradeUK.pdf

[11] "Would Prescription Drug Importation Reduce U.S. Spending?," Congressional Budget Office, April 29, 2004, http://www.cbo.gov/ftpdocs/54xx/doc5406/04-29-PrescriptionDrugs.pdf and Becky Bright, "Most Americans Support Legalizing Drug Imports

From Canada, Poll Finds," *The Wall Street Journal*, August 31, 2006. http://online.wsj.com/article/SB115696198593649659. html?mod=health_home_inside_today_left_column

12 Kimberly A. Strassel, "Canadian Drugs, Eh?," *The Wall Street Journal*, May 11, 2007. http://www.opinionjournal.com/columnists/ kstrasselpw/?id=110010064

13 Ibid.

Myth Six

1 New Hampshire and Wisconsin are the two exceptions according to the Insurance Information Institute, August 2008, http://www. iii.org/media/hottopics/insurance/compulsory/

2 Sally C. Pipes, "Is Hillary Clinton's Health Care Plan True Reform? No: Her plan limits, not expands choices," *San Diego Union-Tribune*, October 11, 2007, http://liberty.pacificresearch. org/press/is-hillary-clintons-health-care-proposal-true-reform

3 Sally C. Pipes, "RomneyCare Revisited," *Townhall*, November 15, 2007, http://liberty.pacificresearch.org/press/romneycare-revisited

4 Reed Abelson, "Small Business Is Latest Focus In Health Fight," *New York Times*, July 10, 2008.

5 Robert Steinbrook, "Health Care Reform in Massachusetts -- Expanding Coverage, Escalating Costs," *New England Journal of Medicine*, 358:2757-2760, no. 26, June 26, 2008.

6 Sally C. Pipes, "RomneyCare Revisited."

7 Sally C. Pipes, "Universally Bad," *National Review*, October 18, 2007, http://liberty.pacificresearch.org/press/universally-bad

8 Robert Steinbrook, "Health Care Reform in Massachusetts."

9 Ibid.

10 Ibid.

11 Ibid.

12 Grace-Marie Turner, "Massachusetts Miracle—or Mess," Galen Institute, July 14, 2008.

13 Alice Dembner, "Cost of health initiative up $400m," *The Boston Globe*, January 24, 2008, http://www.boston.com/news/local/articles/2008/01/24/cost_of_health_initiative_up_400m/

14 Robert Steinbrook, "Health Care Reform in Massachusetts."
15 Grace-Marie Turner, Address to the Alliance for Health Reform, May 19, 2008.
16 Ibid.
17 Robert Steinbrook, "Health Care Reform in Massachusetts."
18 Merrill Matthews, "Is Romney's Health Care Plan Conservative?" *Human Events*, December 27, 2007.
19 See, Glen Whitman, "Hazards of the Individual Health Care Mandate," CATO, Sept/Oct, 2007: http://www.cato.org/pubs/policy_report/v29n5/cpr29n5-1.html
20 Robert Steinbrook, "Health Care Reform in Massachusetts."
21 Cynthia McCormick, "Health insurance penalties announced by state," *Cape Cod Times*, January 5, 2008, http://www.capecodonline.com/apps/pbcs.dll/article?AID=/20080105/NEWS/801050331/-1/LIFE03
22 Sally C. Pipes, "Universally Bad."
23 John R. Graham, "From Heart Transplants to Hairpieces: The Questionable Benefits of State Benefit Mandates for Health Insurance," (San Francisco, California: The Pacific Research Institute, July 21, 2008), http://liberty.pacificresearch.org/press/state-health-benefit-mandates-increase-the-number-of-uninsured
24 Victoria Craig Bunce, J.P. Wieske, and Vlasta Prikazsky, "Health Insurance Mandates in the States, 2007," (Alexandria, Virginia: Council for Affordable Health Insurance, 2007), http://www.cahi.org/cahi_contents/resources/pdf/MandatesInTheStates2007.pdf
25 John R. Graham, "From Heart Transplants to Hairpieces."
26 Ibid.
27 Sally C. Pipes, "Universally Bad."
28 Ibid.
29 Tom Chorneau and Christopher Heredia, "Record numbers of Californians living without health insurance," *San Francisco Chronicle*, August 29, 2007, http://www.sfgate.com/cgi-bin/article.cgi?file=/c/a/2007/08/29/MN91RR0GB.DTL
30 "Massachusetts-Style Coverage Expansion: What Would It Cost in California?" (Oakland, California: California HealthCare Foundation, April, 2006), http://www.chcf.org/topics/healthinsurance/index.cfm?itemID=120742

[31] Sally C. Pipes, "Is Hillary Clinton's Health Care Plan True Reform?"

Myth Seven

[1] "Remarks of Senator Barack Obama," *New York Times*, May 29, 2007, http://www.nytimes.com/2007/05/29/us/politics/28text-obama.html?pagewanted=all

[2] "Remarks By John McCain On Health Care on Day Two of the 'Call to Action Tour,'" McCain–Palin official website, April 29, 2008, http://www.johnmccain.com/informing/news/speeches/2c3cfa3a-748e-4121-84db-28995cf367da.htm

[3] *The Power of Prevention*, (Washington DC: U.S. Department of Health and Human Services, 2003), http://www.healthierus.gov/STEPS/summit/prevportfolio/power/index.html; U.S. Representative Tom Udall, Statement of Introduction for the Healthy Workforce Act of 2007, October 2, 2007, http://www.tomudall.house.gov/index.php?option=com_content&task=view&id=295&Itemid=1

[4] "Overweight and Obesity," Centers for Disease Control and Prevention, May 22, 2007, http://www.cdc.gov/nccdphp/dnpa/obesity/economic_consequences.htm

[5] "Smoking and Tobacco Use" Centers for Disease Control and Prevention, July, 2007, http://www.cdc.gov/tobacco/data_statistics/fact_sheets/economics/economic_facts.htm

[6] Coined by Jay Leno. Cited in, Diana M. Ernst, "Why Fat Laws Fail," *Sacramento Union*, November 2, 2007, http://liberty.pacificresearch.org/press/why-fat-laws-fail

[7] Ian Mount, "Would you eat 2,900-calorie cheese fries?" CNNMoney.com, April 29, 2008, http://money.cnn.com/2008/04/24/smbusiness/full_disclosure_menu.fsb/index.htm

[8] Ibid.

[9] "Overview List—How many Smokefree Laws?" American Non-smokers' Rights Foundation, 2008, http://www.no-smoke.org/pdf/mediaordlist.pdf

[10] "England smoking ban takes effect," BBC News, July 1, 2007. Kenya: "Kenya moves to ban public smoking," *BBC News*, May

31, 2005, http://news.bbc.co.uk/2/hi/africa/4595309.stm Uruguay: "Uruguay curbs smoking in public," *BBC News*, March 1, 2006, http://news.bbc.co.uk/2/hi/americas/4761624.stm Slovenia: "Slovenia Gets Tough Anti-Smoking Legislation," Government Communication Office, Republic of Slovenia, June 26, 2007, http://www.ukom.gov.si/eng/slovenia/publications/slovenia-news/4994/5005/ Virginia: Exerpts from Rosalind S. Helderman, "VA Senate Passes Indoor Smoking Ban," *The Washington Post*, February 14, 2006, (Washington DC: Action on Smoking and Health) http://www.no-smoking.org/Feb06/02-14-06-1.html

[11] Rachel Martin, "Global Anti-Smoking Initiative Gets Huge Financial Boost," ABC News, July 27, 2008, http://www.abcnews.go.com/Health/story?id=5459812&page=1

[12] www.Scribd.com, September 6, 2008, http://209.85.173.104/search?q=cache:Pni-bEppeHcJ:www.scribd.com/doc/191827/hillary-clinton-2008-healthcare-costs+hillary+clinton+drivers+of+health+care+costs+prevention&hl=en&ct=clnk&cd=1&gl=us <http://209.85.173.104/search?q=cache:Pni-bEppeHcJ:www.scribd.com/doc/191827/hillary-clinton-2008-healthcare-costs+hillary+clinton+drivers+of+health+care+costs+prevention&hl=en&ct=clnk&cd=1&gl=us>

[13] Newt Gingrich and Mike Huckabee, "Healthy Americans Mean a Healthy America," *RealClearPolitics*, August 11, 2007, http://www.realclearpolitics.com/articles/2007/08/healthy_americans_mean_a_healt.html

[14] In 1995, 16 percent of Americans were obese. In 2007, 26 percent of Americans were obese. (http://apps.nccd.cdc.gov/brfss/)

[15] W. Kip Viscusi, "The New Cigarette Paternalism," *Regulation*, Winter, 2002-2003, www.cato.org/pubs/regulation/regv25n4/v25n4-13.pdf

[16] W.Kip Viscusi, *Smoking: Making the Risky Decision*, New York: Oxford University Press, 1992, 77.

[17] W. Kip Viscusi, "The New Cigarette Paternalism."

[18] "State Excise Tax Rates on Cigarettes," Federation of Tax Administrators, January 1, 2008, http://www.taxadmin.org/FTA/rate/cigarett.html

[19] W. Kip Viscusi, "The New Cigarette Paternalism."

[20] Cited in Tom Farley and Deborah A. Cohen, *Prescription for a Healthy Nation*, Boston, Beacon Press, 2005, p. 133.

[21] California Senate Bill 677, Introduced by Senator Ortiz, February 21, 2003, http://www.leginfo.ca.gov/pub/03-04/bill/sen/sb_0651-0700/sb_677_bill_20030221_introduced.html

[22] "Special Report: Soda Ban Lacks Scientific Fizz," The Center for Consumer Freedom, June 5, 2003, http://www.consumerfreedom.com/news_detail.cfm/headline/1953

[23] David S Ludwig, Karen E Peterson, Steven L Gortmaker, "Relation between consumption of sugar-sweetened drinks and childhood obesity: a prospective, observational analysis," *The Lancet*, 357, February 17, 2001, 508, http://epsl.asu.edu/ceru/Documents/lancet.pdf

[24] John P. Foreyt, "Weight Loss: Counseling and Long-term Management," *Medscape Today*, November 11, 2004

[25] Sally C. Pipes, "Brave New Diet," *The Washington Post*, December 26, 2007, http://www.washingtonpost.com/wp-dyn/content/article/2007/12/25/AR2007122500862.html

[26] Ibid.

[27] "Obesity Death Rate Lower Than Thought," Associated Press, April 20, 2005.

[28] Body-mass index stats, The Center for Consumer Freedom, http://consumerfreedom.com/bmiscale/stats.html

[29] Luc Bonneux, Jan J Barendregt, Wilma J Nusselder, Paul J Van der Maas, "Preventing fatal diseases increases healthcare costs: cause elimination life table approach," *BMJ*, 316, January 3, 1998, 26-29, http://www.bmj.com/cgi/content/abstract/316/7124/26

[30] "Study: Fat people cheaper to treat," *USA Today*, February 5, 2008, http://www.usatoday.com/news/health/2008-02-05-obese-cost_N.htm, Citing this paper: Pieter H. M. van Baal, *et.al*, "Lifetime Medical Costs of Obesity: Prevention No Cure for Increasing Health Expenditure," *PloS Medicine*, February 5, 2008, http://medicine.plosjournals.org/archive/1549-1676/5/2/pdf/10.1371_journal.pmed.0050029-L.pdf

[31] Joshua T. Cohen, Peter J. Neumann and Milton C. Weinstein, "Does Preventive Care Save Money? Health Economics and the

Presidential Candidates," *New England Journal of Medicine*, 358, 661-663, http://content.nejm.org/cgi/content/full/358/7/661

32 Pieter H. M. van Baal, *et.al*, "Lifetime Medical Costs of Obesity: Prevention No Cure for Increasing Health Expenditure," Plos Medicine, February 5, 2008, http://medicine.plosjournals.org/archive/1549-1676/5/2/pdf/10.1371_journal.pmed.0050029-L.pdf

33 Arthur D. Little Inc., "Public Finance Balance of Smoking in the Czech Republic," Philip Morris CR, November 28, 2000, http://www.tobaccofreekids.org/reports/philipmorris/pmczechstudy.pdf

34 Pieter H. M. van Baal, *et.al*, "Lifetime Medical Costs of Obesity."

35 "Shake-up for takeaway salt cellar," *BBC News*, February 2, 2008, http://news.bbc.co.uk/2/hi/uk_news/wales/north_east/7222466.stm

36 Abraham Lincoln (1809–65), speech, December 18, 1840, to Illinois House of Representatives.

Myth Eight

1 "Poverty: 2006 Highlights," (Washington DC: U.S. Census Bureau, 2006), http://www.census.gov/hhes/www/poverty/poverty06/pov06hi.html

2 "Historical Poverty Tables," (Washington DC: U.S. Census Bureau), http://www.census.gov/hhes/www/poverty/histpov/hst-pov2.html

3 Ibid.

4 John S. O'Shea, "More Medicaid Means Less Quality Health Care," Heritage Foundation, WebMemo #1402, http://www.heritage.org/Research/HealthCare/wm1402.cfm; Grace-Marie Turner, "Moving Forward on Medicaid," The Galen Institute, January 22, 2008, http://www.galen.org/component,8/action,show_content/id,13/blog_id,998/category_id,15/type,33/. (According to CMS website: "More than 46.0 million persons received health care services through the Medicaid program in FY 2001 (the last year for which beneficiary data are available)." http://www.cms.hhs.gov/MedicaidGenInfo/03_TechnicalSummary.asp#TopOfPage

5 "Medicare at a Glance," *The Miami Herald*, August 3, 2008, http://www.miamiherald.com/news/more-info/story/627481.html

6   Office of Management and Budget, *Budget of the United States Government*, Fiscal Year 2006, (Washington DC: Department of Health and Human Services), 137, http://www.whitehouse.gov/omb/budget/fy2006/hhs.html

7   James E. Calvin, Matthew T. Roe, Anita Y. Chen, *et. al*, "Insurance Coverage and Care of Patients with Non-ST Segment Elevation Acute Coronary Syndrome," *Annals of Internal Medicine*, 145 no. 10, November 21, 2006, 739-748, http://www.annals.org/cgi/content/abstract/145/10/739

8   Peter J. Cunningham and Jessica H. May, "Medicaid Patients Increasingly Concentrated Among Physicians," Center for Studying Health Systems Change, Tracking Report 16, August 2006.

9   MEDPAC, "Access to Care in the Medicare Program," *Data Book*, June 2004, 42.

10 Peter J. Cunningham and Len M. Nichols, "The Effects of Medicaid Reimbursement on the Access to Care of Medicaid Enrollees: A Community Perspective," *Medical Care Research and Review*, 62, no. 6, December 2005.

11 Vanessa Fuhrmans, "Note to Medicaid Patients: The Doctor Won't See You," *The Wall Street Journal*, July 19, 2007, p. A1.

12 Jennifer N. Edwards, Michelle M. Doty, and Cathy Schoen, "The Erosion of Employer-Based Health Coverage and the Threat to Workers' Health Care: Findings from The Commonwealth Fund 2002 Workplace Health Insurance Survey," The Commonwealth Fund, *Issue Brief*, August 2002), p.7, http://www.cmwf.org/usr_doc/edwards_erosion.pdf

13 Tim Novak and Chris Fusco, "U of C shnning poor patients?" *Chicago Sun Times*, August 23, 2008.

14 Grace-Marie Turner, "Moving Forward on Medicaid," The Galen Institute, January 22, 2008, http://www.galen.org/component,8/action,show_content/id,13/blog_id,998/category_id,15/type,33/

15 John S. O'Shea, "More Medicaid Means Less Quality Health Care," The Heritage Foundation WebMemo #1402, March 21, 2007), http://www.heritage.org/Research/HealthCare/wm1402.cfm

16 Nina Owcharenko, "Florida and South Carolina: Two Serious Efforts to Improve Medicaid," Heritage Foundation , WebMemo

#920, (Washington DC:, November 18, 2005), http://www.heritage.org/Research/HealthCare/wm920.cfm

17 "Population," Federal Interagency Forum on Aging Related Statistics, http://agingstats.gov/agingstatsdotnet/Main_Site/Data/2008_Documents/Population.aspx

18 Nina Owcharenko, "The Medicaid Regulations: Stopping the Abuse of Taxpayers' Dollars," The Heritage Foundation, Web-Memo #1911, Washington DC, May 2, 2008), http://www.heritage.org/Research/HealthCare/wm1911.cfm

19 Kathryn G. Allen, "Medicaid: Intergovernmental Transfers Have Facilitated State Financing Schemes," Testimony Before the Subcommittee on Health, Committee on Energy and Commerce, House of Representatives, Government Accountability Office, March 18, 2004, http://www.gao.gov/new.items/d04574t.pdf

20 Ibid.

21 Ibid.

22 Ibid.

23 http://www.cbsnews.com/stories/2006/10/05/fyi/main2067346.shtml?source=RSS&attr=_2067346

24 For more information see, "Medicaid: A Brief Summary," Centers for Medicare and Medicaid Services, (Washington DC: U.S. Department of Health and Human Services).

25 Daniel Connolly, "Struggling to just keep TennCare," *Commercial Appeal*, June 29, 2008.

26 Daniel Connolly, "Struggling to just keep TennCare," Commercialappeal.com, June 29, 2008, http://www.aafp.org/online/etc/medialib/aafp_org/documents/policy/state/medicaid-adm-costs.Par.0001.File.tmp/stateadvocacy_MedicaidAdministrativeCosts.pdf

27 Mark Litow and CAHI's Technical Committee, "Rhetoric vs. Reality: Comparing Public and Private Health Care Costs," (Alexandria, Virginia: Council for Affordable Health Insurance, 1994).

28 Steve Jacob, "Long-term care: the issue no candidate is talking about," *Cleveland Plain Dealer*, July 05, 2008, http://blog.cleveland.com/pdopinion/2008/07/longterm_care_the_issue_no_can.html

29 Jeffrey R. Brown and Amy Finkelstein, "The Interaction of Pub-lic and Private Insurance: Medicaid and the Long Term Care Insurance Market," National Bureau of Economic Research, National Bureau of Economic Research Working Paper Series, Working Paper 10989, December 2004, http://www.aei.org/docLib/20050216_BrownFinkelstein.pdf
30 Grace-Marie Turner, "Moving Forward on Medicaid,"The Galen Institute, January 22, 2008, http://www.galen.org/component,8/action,show_content/id,13/blog_id,998/category_id,15/type,33/

Myth Nine

1   President George W. Bush, 2004 State of the Union Address, Washington DC, January 20, 2004, http://www.whitehouse.gov/news/releases/2004/01/20040120-7.html
2   Interview with Newt Gingrich, "Newt Gingrich: healthcare transfor-mation advocate," *Healthcare Financial Management*, September 2006, http://findarticles.com/p/articles/mi_m3257/is_9_60/ai_n16728109
3   According to Wikipedia, "the Commodore 64 was released in August, 1982, at a price of $595." That's about $1,349 in 2008 dollars. The Commodore 64 was the first 64-KB computer to sell for under $600. http://en.wikipedia.org/wiki/Commodore_64 & http://en.wikipedia.org/wiki/Commodore_Plus/4
4   "Push for digital health records," *Baltimore Sun*, June 11, 2008.
5   "Transforming Health Care: The President's Health Information Tech-nology Plan," News and Policies in Focus, White House, http://www.whitehouse.gov/infocus/technology/economic_policy200404/chap3.html
6   Ibid.
7   "Executive Order: Incentives for the Use of Health Information Technology and Establishing the Position of the National Health Information Technology Coordinator," News and Policies, White House, April 27, 2004, http://www.whitehouse.gov/news/releases/2004/04/20040427-4.html
8   John R. Graham, "Keep health data private," *Press-Enterprise*, April 26, 2008, http://www.pe.com/localnews/opinion/localviews/stories/PE_OpEd_Opinion_D_op_0427_graham_loc.2bc6650.html

9   "Rituximab," http://en.wikipedia.org/wiki/Rituxan

10 "Health Information Technology: Can HIT Lower Costs and Improve Quality?" Research Highlights, 2005, RAND Institute, http://www.rand.org/pubs/research_briefs/RB9136/index1.html

11 Gregory Lopes, "Paper still rules patient records: Health-information technology is seen as useful but costly," *Washington Times*, March 5, 2007.

12 "Push for digital health records," *Baltimore Sun*.

13 Ibid.

14 $80 per patient per year: "VA Receives 2006 Innovations in Government Award," United States Office of Veterans Affairs, July 10, 2006), http://www1.va.gov/opa/pressrel/pressrelease.cfm?id=1152; .6 million patients: Kay L. Daly, "Veterans Health Administration: Improvements Needed in Design of Controls over Miscellaneous Obligations," Testimony Before the Subcommittee on Oversight and Investigations, Committee on Veterans' Affairs, House of Representatives, Government Accountability Office, July 31, 2008, http://www.gao.gov/new.items/d081056t.pdf

15 Bill Theobald, "Few doctors, hospitals use electronic health records, study finds," Gannett News Service, October 12, 2006.

16 "Citrix Survey Identifies Need for Strong State Leadership to Meet National Electronic Medical Records Goals," Citrix Systems, Inc., February 19, 2007, http://www.citrix.com/English/NE/news/news.asp?newsID=164385

17 Graham, "Keep health data private."

18 Ibid.

19 Steve Lohr, "U.S. Awards Contracts to Help Automate Health Records," *The New York Times*, November 11, 2005

20 "HHS Secretary Announces 12 Communities Selected to Advance Use of Electronic Health Records in First Ever National Demonstration," (Washington DC: U.S. Department of Health and Human Services, June 10, 2008), http://www.hhs.gov/news/press/2008pres/06/20080610a.html

21 Ben Worthen, "Will a Spoonful of Google Help Cure Health care?" *The Wall Street Journal Online*, February 28, 2008. http://blogs.wsj.com/biztech/2008/02/28/will-a-spoonful-of-google-help-cure-health care/

22 Steve Lohr, "Kaiser Backs Microsoft Patient-Data Plan," *New York Times*, June 10, 2008.

Myth Ten

1 "Core Health Indicators; The latest data from multiple WHO sources," World Health Organization, 2008, http://www.who.int/whosis/database/core/core_select_process.cfm?countries=all&indicators=nha

2 http://select.nytimes.com/2005/11/07/opinion/07krugman.html

3 "Rank Order: Infant mortality rate," *The 2008 World Factbook*, (Washington DC: Central Intelligence Agency, 2008), https://www.cia.gov/library/publications/the-world-factbook/rankorder/2091rank.html (Note that we didn't include the "European Union" as its own nation.)

4 "Rank Order: Life expectancy at birth," *The 2008 World Factbook*, (Washington DC: Central Intelligence Agency, 2008), https://www.cia.gov/library/publications/the-world-factbook/rankorder/2102rank.html (Note that our number ranks the U.S. as where it would fall if the list were comprised solely of UN member states, as the list includes territories (Guam, Puerto Rico, etc) and bodies like the E.U.)

5 *Insuring America's Health: Principles and Recommendations*, The Institute of Medicine, Washington DC, The National Academy Press, 2004, http://www.iom.edu/?id=17848

6 "Canada's Population Clock," Demography division, (Ottawa, Ontario, Statistics Canada, Updated November 30, 2007), http://www.statcan.ca/english/edu/clock/population.htm

7 Nadeem Esmail and Michael Walker, "How Good is Canadian Health Care? 2007" Fraser Institute, November, 2007, http://www.fraserinstitute.org/commerce.web/product_files/HowGood-HC2007rev.pdf

8 Clifford Krauss, "Canada's Private Clinics Surge as Public System Falters," *New York Times*, February 26, 2008, "http://www.nytimes.com/2006/02/28/international/americas/28canada.html?ei=5090&en=ad12dcee61e8b584&ex=1298782800

9   Nadeem Esmail and Michael Walker, "How Good is Canadian Health Care? 2007," Fraser Institute, November, 2007), http://www.fraserinstitute.org/commerce.web/product_files/HowGood-HC2007rev.pdf

10 Nadeem Esmail and Michael Walker, "How Good is Canadian Health Care? 2007"

11 Sally C. Pipes, "Rejecting the Canadian Way," *Real Clear Politics*, May 16, 2006, http://www.realclearpolitics.com/articles/2006/05/rejecting_the_canadian_way.html

12 Clifford Krauss, "Canada's Supreme Court Chips Away at National Health Care," *The New York Times*, June 9 , 2005, http://www.nytimes.com/2005/06/09/international/americas/09cnd-canada.html

13 "In-Depth: Health Care Introduction," CBS News Online, August 22, 2006, http://www.cbc.ca/news/background/healthcare/

14 "Where's leadership on health care?" *National Post*, page A16, June 11, 2005.

15 Susan Delacourt, "Stronach Travels to U.S. for Cancer Treatment," *The Star*, September 14, 2007.

16 Ian Key, "My Cancer Appointment was Cancelled 48 Times," Mirror.co.uk, November 25, 2006, http://www.mirror.co.uk/news/tm_headline=my-cancer-appointment-was-cancelled-48-times-&method=full&objectid=18156184&siteid=94762-name_page.html

17 Dr. Tim Evans, Alberto Mingardi, Dr. Cecile Philippe and Stephen Pollard, "Towards greater partnership in healthcare funding: The rise of health consumerism in British and other European healthcare systems," (Brussels, Belgium: Centre for the New Europe, 2004), http://www.cne.org/pub_pdf/2004_09_00_uk_health.pdf

18 "Waiting lists fall below election level," *BBC News*, March 30, 1999, http://news.bbc.co.uk/1/hi/health/307602.stm

19 "'Sicko': Heavily Doctored, By Kurt Loder," MTV Networks, June 29, 2007, http://www.mtv.com/movies/news/articles/1563758/story.jhtml

20 Dr. Tim Evans, Alberto Mingardi, Dr. Cecile Philippe and Stephen Pollard, "Towards greater partnership in healthcare funding."

21 "Malnutrition Neglected," Country Doctors Association, September 15, 2005, http://www.countrydoctor.co.uk/precis/precis%20-%20Malnutrition%20neglected.htm

22 David Gratzer, "A Canadian Doctor Describes How Socialized Medicine Doesn't Work" *Investor's Business Daily*, July 26, 2007, http://www.ibdeditorials.com/IBDArticles.aspx?id=270338135202343

23 Johnny Munkhammar, speech delivered at the international panel discussion, "Is There a Role for Markets in Health Care?" presented by the International Policy Network and the Galen Institute in Washington, DC, June 14, 2007, http://www.munkhammar.org/blog/pdf/MunkhammarGalenRemarks.doc

24 Johnny Munkhammar:, "America delivers better health care than Europe," *The Washington Examiner*, July 12, 2007, http://www.examiner.com/printa-824602~Johnny_Munkhammar:_America_delivers_better_health_care_than_Europe.html

25 Daniel Martin, "A&E patients left in ambulances for up to FIVE hours 'so trusts can meet government targets,'" *The Daily Mail*, February 18, 2008.

26 Sally C. Pipes, "Coming Soon: Not-So-NICE Health Care?" *Investor's Business Daily*, June 25, 2008, http://www.ibdeditorials.com/IBDArticles.aspx?id=299282658708852

27 Ibid.

28 Sally C. Pipes, "Losing by 'Saving'," *The New York Post*, February 5, 2008, http://www.nypost.com/seven/02052008/postopinion/oped-columnists/losing_by_saving_841252.htm?page=2

29 Ibid.

30 "Europe's Pharmaceutical 'Free Ride' Might Not Be So Free after All; European Drug Prices Are 25-35% Lower Than the U.S.—but a New Study from Bain & Company Suggests Americans Might Be Getting the Better Deal," Business Wire, February 23, 2004, http://findarticles.com/p/articles/mi_m0EIN/is_2004_Feb_23/ai_113529052

31 "Germany's Poor Doctors," 2004 analysis by the National Economic Research Associates, as cited in Der Spiegel. http://www.spiegel.de/img/0,1020,575805,00.jpg

32 Paul Dutton, "The Health Care in France and the United States: Learning from Each Other," (Washington DC: Brookings Institution, July 2002).

33 Johnny Munkhammar:, "America delivers better health care than Europe."

34 David Brown, "Life Expectancy Hits Record High in United States," *The Washington Post*, June 12, 2008, "http://www.washingtonpost.com/wp-dyn/content/article/2008/06/11/AR2008061101570.html?hpid=sec-health

35 "Rate: Number of Crimes per 100,000 Inhabitants," (Clarksburg, Virginia: Crime in the United States, 2005), http://www.fbi.gov/ucr/05cius/data/table_16.html

36 "List of countries by homicide rate," Wikipedia, http://en.wikipedia.org/wiki/List_of_countries_by_homicide_rate#cite_note-winslow-interpol-pakistan-40 (Each stat is sourced with a more appropriate source on the Wikipedia page.)

37 "National Statistics:Table Updated with 2006 Final Data and 2007 Annual Data," Fatality Analysis Reporting System Encyclopedia, http://www-fars.nhtsa.dot.gov/Main/index.aspx

38 "Myths and Facts," BigGovHealth, Center for Medicine in the Public Interest, 2008, http://www.biggovhealth.org/resource/myths-facts/

39 Robert L. Ohsfeldt and John E. Schneider, *The Business of Health: The Role of Competition, Markets, and Regulation*, Washington, DC, AEI Press, October 3, 2006, http://www.aei.org/publications/spubID.24974,filter.all/pub_detail.asp; David Gratzer, "A Canadian Doctor Describes How Socialized Medicine Doesn't Work" *Investor's Business Daily*, July 26, 2007, http://ibdeditorials.com/IBDArticles.aspx?id=270338135202343

40 N. Gregory Mankiw, "Beyond Those Health Care Numbers," *The New York Times*, November 4, 2007, http://www.nytimes.com/2007/11/04/business/04view.html?_r=2&adxnnl=1&oref=slogin&ref=business&adxnnlx=1217851257-7nWTn5MwZIt8rz-pUMnTlBg

41 Postgraduate Research Training in Reproductive Health Fudan University, Shanghai Questions and answers, What is the definition of live birth?" (Geneva, Switzerland: The Geneva Foundation for Medical Education and Research), http://www.gfmer.ch/Medical_education_En/Live_birth_definition.htm

42 "The Court of cassation reminds the status of lifeless children," Gene Ethique, (Paris, France: Jérôme Lejeune Foundation, March, 2007), http://www.genethique.org/en/letters/letters/2008/march.htm

43 David Hogberg, "Don't Fall Prey to Propaganda: Life Expectancy and Infant Mortality are Unreliable Measures for Comparing the U.S. Health Care System to Others," National Policy Analysis (Washington DC: The National Center for Public Policy Research, July, 2006), http://www.nationalcenter.org/NPA547ComparativeHealth.html

44 Bernadine Healy, "Behind the Baby Count," *U.S. News and World Report*, September 24, 2006, http://health.usnews.com/usnews/health/articles/060924/2healy.htm

45 "World Health Organization Assesses the World's Health Systems," *The World Health Report*, June 21, 2000, http://www.who.int/whr/2000/media_centre/press_release/en/index.html

46 Glen Whitman, "WHO's Fooling Who? The World Health Organization's Problematic Ranking of Health Care Systems," (Washington DC: CATO Institute, February 28, 2008), http://www.cato.org/pubs/bp/bp101.pdf

47 "World Health Organization Assesses the World's Health Systems," *The World Health Report*, June 21, 2000, http://www.who.int/whr/2000/media_centre/press_release/en/index.html

48 Michelle Lang "Calgary's quads: Born in the U.S.A." *Calgary Herald*, August 17, 2007.

49 David Gratzer, "American Cancer Care Beats the Rest," *The Wall Street Journal*, July 22, 2008, http://online.wsj.com/article/SB121668625082172105.html?mod=googlenews_wsj

50 Devon Herrick, "FYI: We're number One. Again!" John Goodman's Health Policy Blog, July 30, 2008, http://www.john-goodman-blog.com/were-number-one-again/

51 Jane Sarasohn-Kahn "The Value of Medical Innovation - personal, global, fiscal," THINK-health, October 2, 2007, http://www.health-populi.com/2007/10/value-of-medical-innovation-personal.html

52 Kevin M. Murphy and Robert Topel, "Introduction," *Measuring the Gains from Medical Research: An Economic Approach*, Chicago, Illinois, University of Chicago Press, 2002.

53 Doug Bandow, "Saving Pennies, Costing Lives," *The Wall Street Journal Europe*, March 16, 2005.

54 Sarah-Kate Templeton, "NHS Threat to halt care for cancer patient." *The Sunday Times*, December 16, 2007.

55   Antonia Maioni, "The Castonguay Report."
56   David Gratzer, "Canadian Health Care We So Envy Lies
      In Ruins, Its Architect Admits," *Investor's Business Daily*,
      June 25, 2008, http://www.ibdeditorials.com/IBDArticles.
      aspx?id=299282509335931
57   Antonia Maioni, "The Castonguay Report."
58   Richard Smith, "The private sector in the English NHS: from pariah
      to saviour in under a decade," Canadian Medical Association Jour-
      nal, August 2, 2005, http://www.cmaj.ca/cgi/content/full/173/3/273

Solutions

1   The President's Advisory Panel on Federal Tax Reform, The
      Panel's Recommendations, Chapter Five, November 1, 2005,
      http://taxreformpanel.gov/final-report/TaxReform_Ch5.pdf
2   Victoria Craig Bunce and JP Wieske, Health Insurance Mandates
      in the States 2008, (Alexandria, Virginia: Council for Afford-
      able Health Insurance, 2008, http://www.cahi.org/cahi_contents/
      resources/pdf/HealthInsuranceMandates2008.pdf
3   "America's Health Insurance Plans Janurary 2008, Census Shows
      6.1 Million People Covered by High Deductible Health Plans,"
      (Washington DC, American's Health Insurance Plans, April,
      2008) http://www.ahipresearch.org/pdfs/2008_HSA_Census.pdf
4   Grace Marie Turner, "Customer Health Care," *The Wall
      Street Journal*, March 14, 2007, http://online.wsj.com/article/
      SB117911344481901660.html
5   Grace Marie Turner, "Customer Health Care," *The Wall
      Street Journal*, March 14, 2007, http://online.wsj.com/article/
      SB117911344481901660.html
6   "Retail Health Clinics Popular for Kids," CBS News, April 20,
      2007, http://www.cbsnews.com/stories/2007/04/20/health/webmd/
      main2710222.shtml
7   "AMA Calls for Investigation of Retail Health Clinics," *Medical
      News Today*, June 26, 2007.

About the Author

Sally C. Pipes is president and chief executive officer of the Pacific Research Institute, a San Francisco-based think tank founded in 1979. Prior to becoming president in 1991, she was assistant director of the Fraser Institute, based in Vancouver, Canada.

Ms. Pipes addresses national and international audiences on health care, women's issues, and the economy. She has been interviewed on CNN's *Glenn Beck Show*; NBC's *Nightly News with Brian Williams*; CNNfn; *The O'Reilly Factor*, FOX News; *Your World With Neil Cavuto, The Today Show*; *Kudlow & Company* on CNBC, *Dateline*; *Politically Incorrect*; *The Dennis Miller Show*; and other prominent programs.

She has written regular columns for *Chief Executive* and *Investor's Business Daily*. Currently, she writes a monthly column on health care issues for the *Examiner* newspapers. Her opinion pieces have appeared in the *Wall Street Journal, Washington Post, USA Today, Financial Times of London, The Hill, RealClearPolitics, New York Times, Los Angeles Times, San Francisco Chronicle, Sacramento Bee, New York Daily News*, the *Boston Globe*, and the *San Diego Union-Tribune*, to name a few. Ms. Pipes' views on health care appeared in a special report of the world's 30 leading health care experts published by *Forbes.com* entitled, "Solutions: Health Care. She was quoted in *Shape* Magazine for her support of Consumer Directed Health Care.

Ms. Pipes writes, speaks, debates, and gives invited testimony at the national and state levels on key health care issues facing America. Topics include the false promise of a single-payer system as exists in Canada, pharmaceutical pricing, solving the problem of the uninsured, and strategies for consumer-driven health care. In September 2008, Ms. Pipes debated Paul Krugman, Nobel laureate, Princeton economics professor, and *New York Times* columnist, in New York at Rockefeller University. She was on the opposing side of the motion "Universal Health Coverage is the Responsibility of the Federal Government." Sponsored by Intelligence Squared, the debate was attended by 450 people and will be viewed by 270 million around the world through NPR and BBC Worldwide. She was one of Mayor Rudy Giuliani's four health care advisors in his bid for the Republican nomination for president. She appears in Michael Moore's movie "Sicko" and has participated in prominent debates and public forums, testified before five committees of the California and Oregon legislatures, appeared on popular television programs, participated in talk radio shows nationwide, and had 127 opeds published on health care issues in 2007.

Her book, *Miracle Cure: How to Solve America's Health Care Crisis and Why Canada Isn't the Answer* with a foreword by Milton Friedman was released September 2004. It is available on Amazon.com. Hillsdale College published her essay on health care reform in the 2006 edition of *Champions of Freedom*. It was part of a conference on "Entrepreneurship and the Spirit of America". She also co-authored with Spencer Star *Income and Taxation in Canada* and co-authored with Michael Walker seven editions of *Tax Facts*.

Ms. Pipes has held a variety of positions in both the private and public sectors. In British Columbia, the Ministry of Consumer and Corporate Affairs appointed her director and vice-chairman of the Financial Institutions Commission.

Ms. Pipes served on the Medical Advisory Council of Genworth Financial's Long-Term Care Insurance Division in 2006, the national advisory board of Capital Research Center, the advisory board for the Bastiat Journalism Prize, the board of advisors of the San Francisco Lawyers Chapter of the Federalist Society, the Advisory Board of the California Association of Scholars, and the State Policy Network president's advisory council. She has served as a trustee of St. Luke's Hospital Foundation in San Francisco, a board member of the Independent Women's Forum, and as a governor of the Donner Canadian Foundation. She was a member of California Governor Arnold Schwarzenegger's transition team in 2003-04.

She received the Roe Award at the 2004 annual meeting of State Policy Network. The award is a tribute to an individual in the state public policy movement who has a passion for liberty, a willingness to work for it, and noteworthy achievement in turning dreams into realities. In 2005, she was named one of the Top 10 Women in the Conservative Movement in America as published by *Human Events*. In 2008, she was honored by the California Women's Leadership Association. She received the 3rd Annual Women Achievers' award, "Celebrating the Spirit of Women". She was also featured in a new book "Women Who Paved the Way" as one of 35 most outstanding women in business in the nation.

Ms. Pipes, who became an American citizen in 2006, is a member of the Mont Pelerin Society. While in Canada she was a member of the Canadian Association for Business Economics (president for two terms).

About the Pacific Research Institute

The Pacific Research Institute (PRI) champions freedom, opportunity, and personal responsibility by advancing free-market policy solutions. It provides practical solutions for the policy issues that impact the daily lives of all Americans, and demonstrates why the free market is more effective than the government at providing the important results we all seek: good schools, quality health care, a clean environment, and a robust economy.

Founded in 1979 and based in San Francisco, PRI is a non-profit, non-partisan organization supported by private contributions. Its activities include publications, public events, media commentary, community leadership, legislative testimony, and academic outreach.

Education Studies
PRI works to restore to all parents the basic right to choose the best educational opportunities for their children. Through research and grassroots outreach, PRI promotes parental choice in education, high academic standards, teacher quality, charter schools, and school-finance reform.

Business and Economic Studies
PRI shows how the entrepreneurial spirit—the engine of economic growth and opportunity—is stifled by onerous taxes, regulations,

and litigation. It advances policy reforms that promote a robust economy, consumer choice, and innovation.

Health Care Studies
PRI proposes market-based reforms that would improve affordability, access, quality, and consumer choice. PRI also demonstrates why a single-payer, Canadian model would be detrimental to the health care of all Americans.

Technology Studies
PRI advances policies to defend individual liberty, foster high-tech growth and innovation, and
limit regulation.

Environmental Studies
PRI reveals the dramatic and long-term trend toward a cleaner, healthier environment. It also examines and promotes the essential ingredients for abundant resources and environmental quality: property rights, markets, local action, and private initiative.